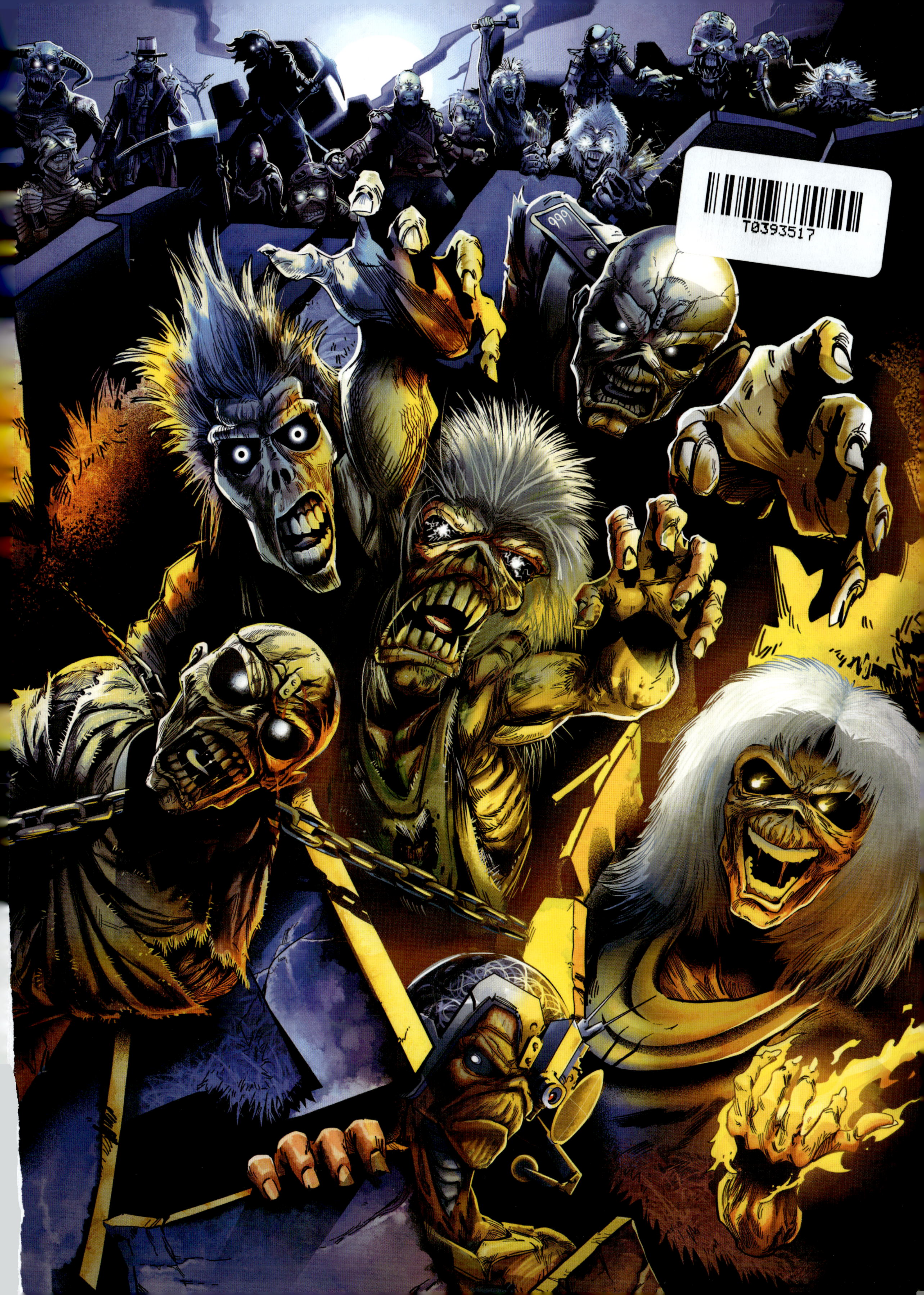

WHERE IS EDDIE?

CREATED AT FANTOONS ANIMATION STUDIOS

ART DIRECTOR: DAVID CALCANO

ADDITIONAL ART DIRECTORS: ITTAI MANERO
JONATAS TOBIAS

WRITTEN BY: EDUARDO BENATAR
LINDSAY LEE
SAMUEL BLANCO

ILLUSTRATED BY: JORGE MANSILLA
JUAN RIERA
LARISSA RIVERO
LINDSAY LEE
SAMUEL BLANCO

COLORED BY: ALBERTO BELANDRIA
CATHERIN CHINEA
JORGE MANSILLA
LINDSAY LEE
SAMUEL BLANCO

LETTERING AND GRAPHIC DESIGN: CATHERIN CHINEA
EDUARDO BRAUN

EDITED BY: BETH SCORZATO

EXECUTIVE PRODUCER: LINDA OTERO

PRODUCER: MARIAFERNANDA FUENTES

BOOK LAYOUT DESIGNER: BRETT BURNER

Sales: info@fantoons.tv / www.fantoons.tv / www.ironmaiden.com

Iron Maiden Where is Eddie? © 2023 Fantoons LLC. All Rights Reserved.
© 2023 Iron Maiden LLP. Iron Maiden ® Under License to Global Merchandising Services Ltd

No part of this publication may be reproduced, distributed or transmitted in any form or by any means, electronic, mechanical, photocopying or otherwise, without prior permission of the author.

Printed in China.   ISBN: 978-1-970047-33-2
First Paperback Edition 2025

FANTOONS

IRON MAIDEN IS GONNA GET YOU

True words indeed. When I was a teenager in the 90s, and starting to be interested in music, concerts from big international bands were a very rare thing in my native Venezuela. But in October 1992, the unthinkable happened: Iron Maiden played two sold out shows in Caracas. Watching these incredible musicians perform was an unforgettable experience, and I was sold. Fast forward to now, I'm still a fan, and Maiden is more relevant than ever, filling stadiums on every continent and usually getting there by flying their own plane. Accompanied, of course, by the most famous character in rock. I don't have to tell you his name!

Their cinematic and literary references in their lyrics, and the atmospheres their music can create, were the perfect inspiration for this book. I hope you enjoy exploring it as much as we did working on it, and please take your time on each page. It's not just Eddie you should be looking for...there are many Easter eggs...see how many you can spot.

And remember to realize you are living in the golden years!

EDUARDO BENATAR

IRON MAIDEN
WHERE IS EDDIE?

IRON MAIDEN
The Eddie that we learned to both love and fear, originating from their first album cover.

KILLERS
From the second album cover, bloody axe and all.

THE NUMBER OF THE BEAST
The same Eddie that either controls the devil or decapitates him, as he does on the single.

PIECE OF MIND
Straight from both the asylum and the album cover.

2 MINUTES TO MIDNIGHT
Soldier Eddie sans machine gun, from the single cover.

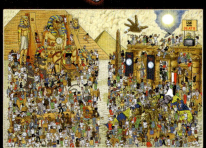

POWERSLAVE
This mummy Eddie graced the cover of the World Slavery tour book and appeared with the band onstage during that time.

SOMEWHERE IN TIME
This Eddie is from the album cover, but also appears on the single for Stranger in a Strange Land (with some badass clothing, we might say).

SEVENTH SON OF A SEVENTH SON
Also from the amazing cover of the album, but look for some single cover references.

FEAR OF THE DARK
This Eddie can be seen terrorizing a banker on the Be Quick or Be Dead single cover.

THE WICKER MAN
This is the handsome leading man from the video… or maybe one of the crowd.

OUT OF THE SILENT PLANET
From the single cover, here's politician Eddie making promises…we assume.

ROCK IN RIO
This is the menacing Ed Hunter straight from the video game, as well as the name of the tour heralding the return of Bruce and Adrian.

A MATTER OF LIFE AND DEATH
Straight from the Different World single cover, whole planet in hand.

FLIGHT 666
If Bruce isn't flying the plane, this pilot Eddie from the Aces High single should.

BOOK OF SOULS
Ancient Eddie from the cover of the album, ready for a bloody ritual of course.

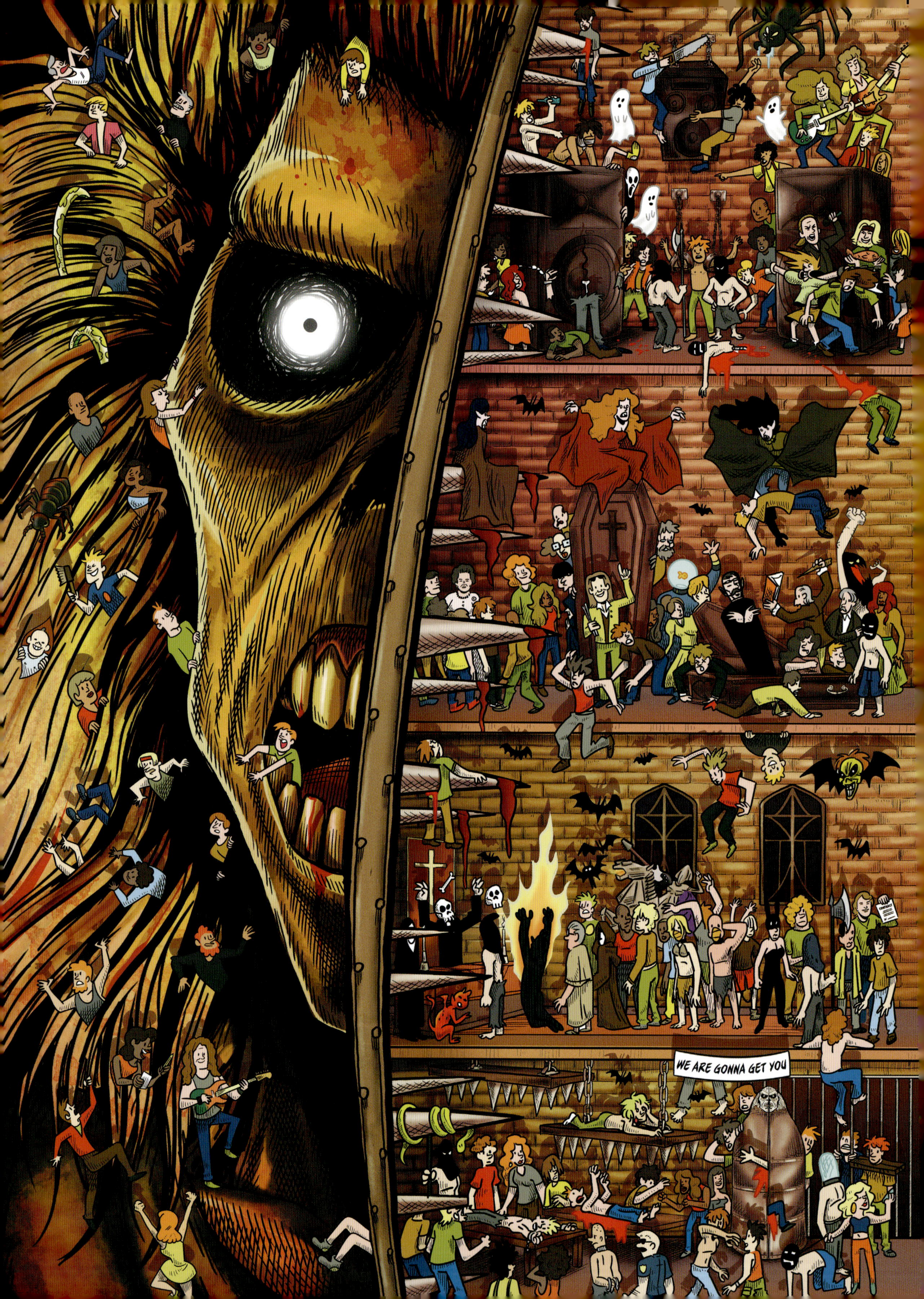
WE ARE GONNA GET YOU

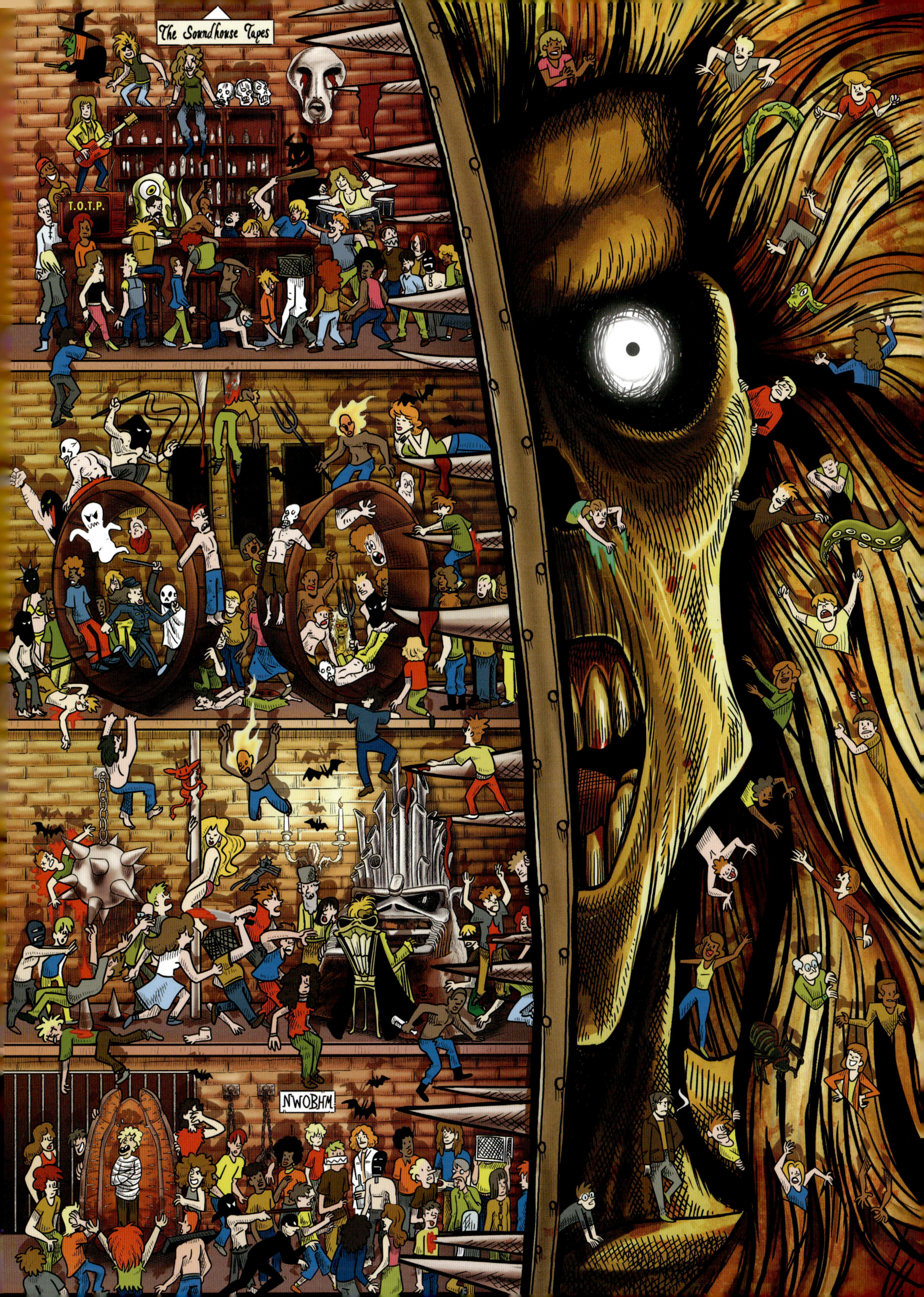
The Soundhouse Tapes
T.O.T.P.
NWOBHM

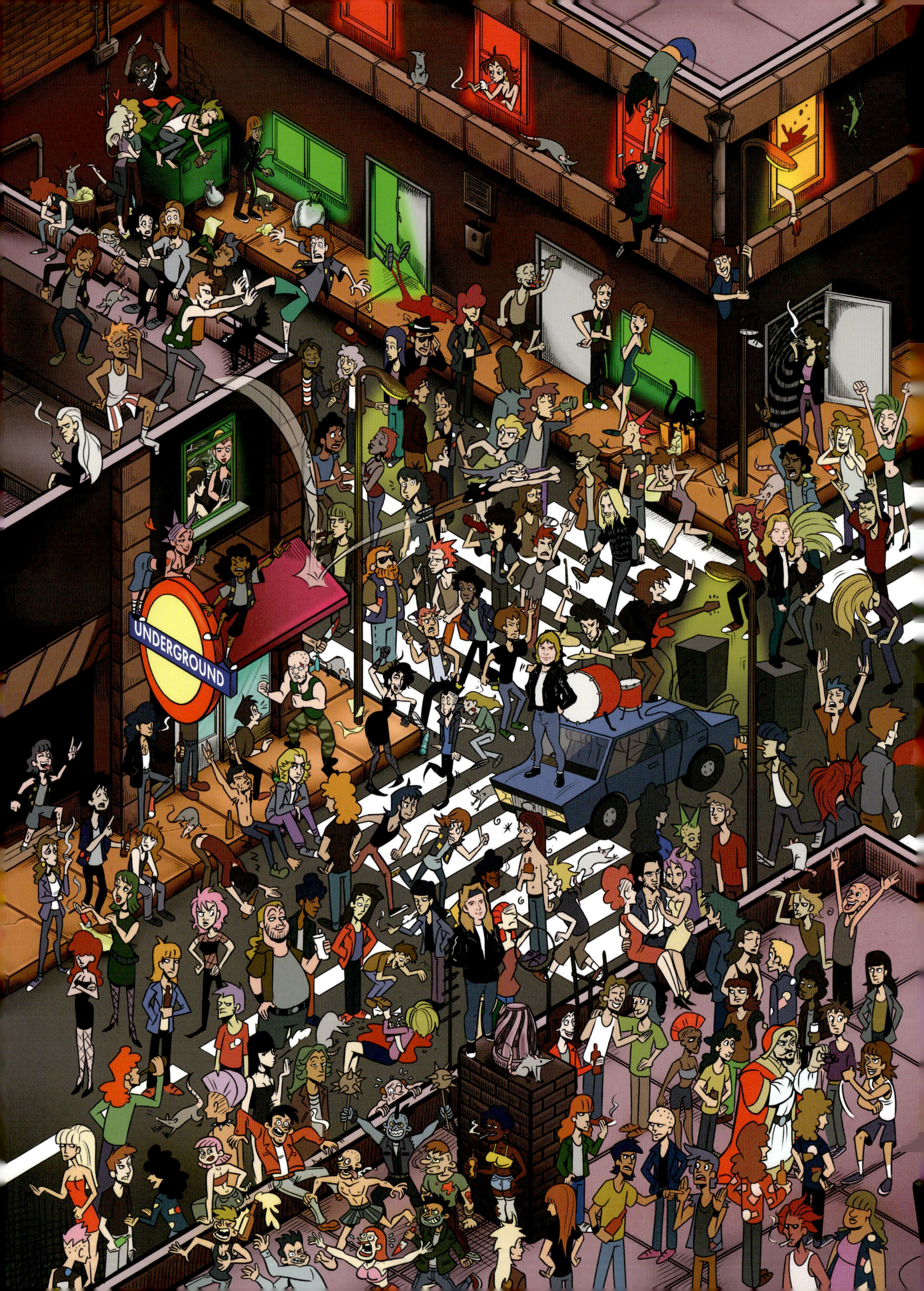
UNDERGROUND

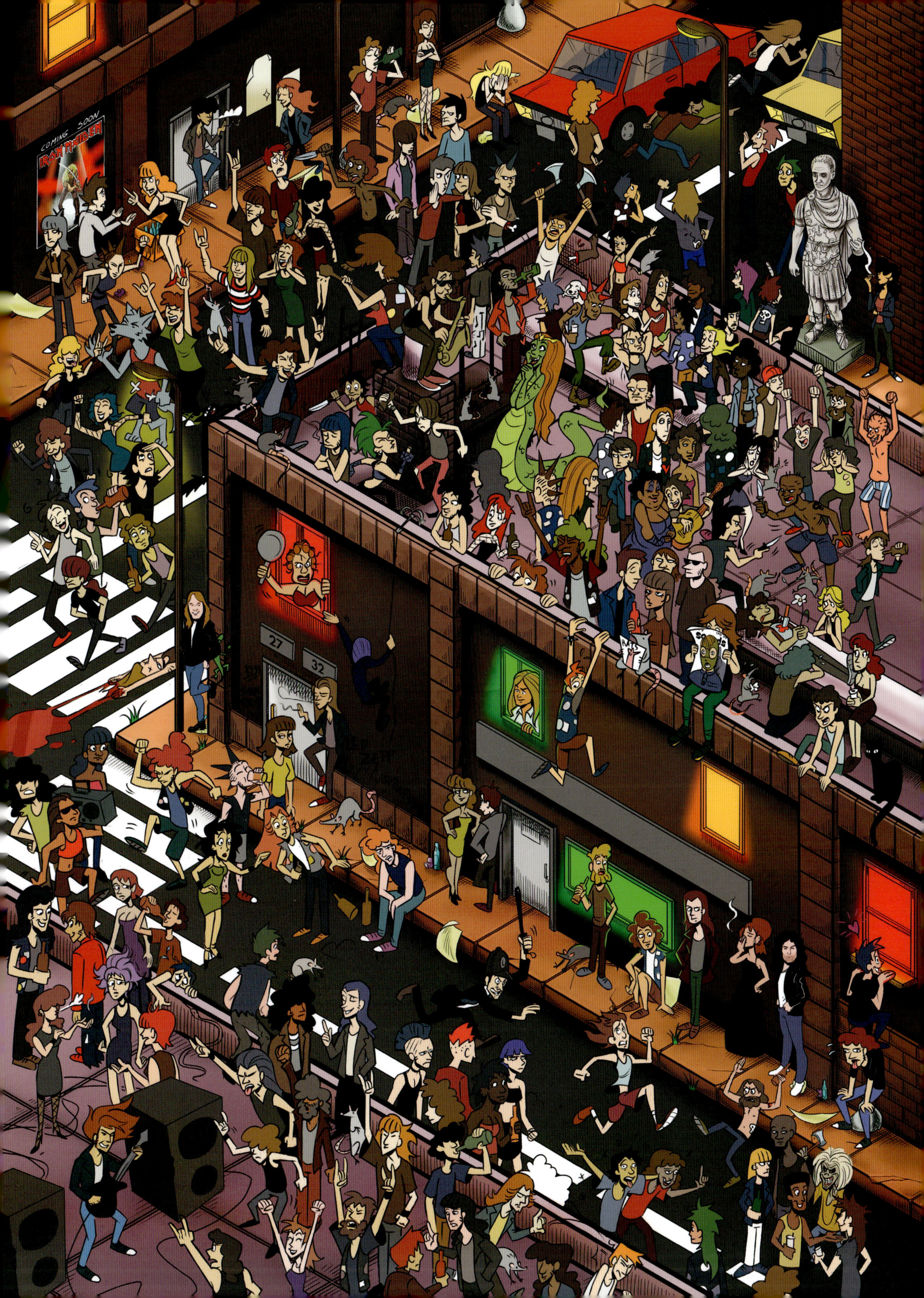
COMING SOON
IRON MAIDEN
27
32

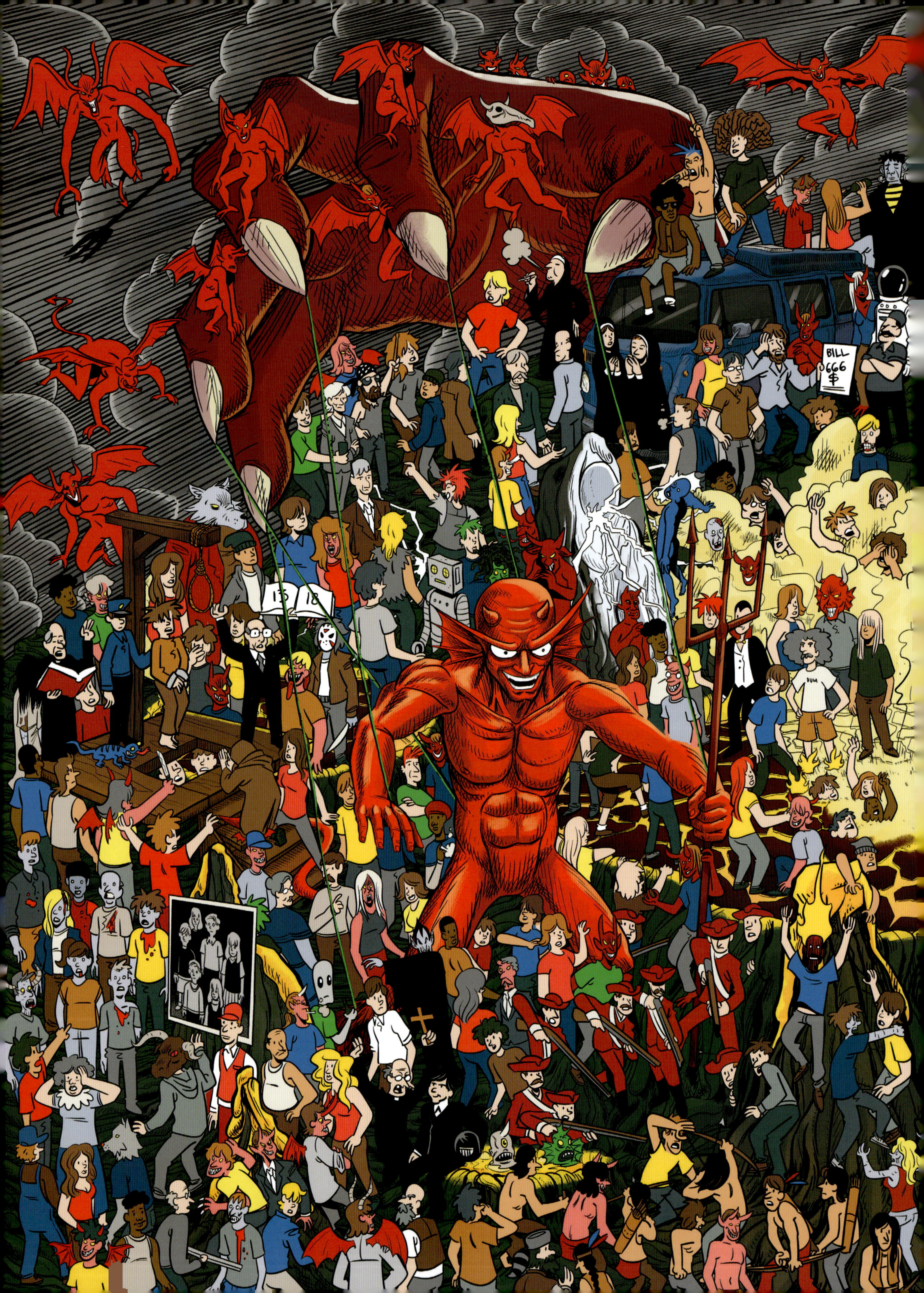
BILL
666
$
DUM

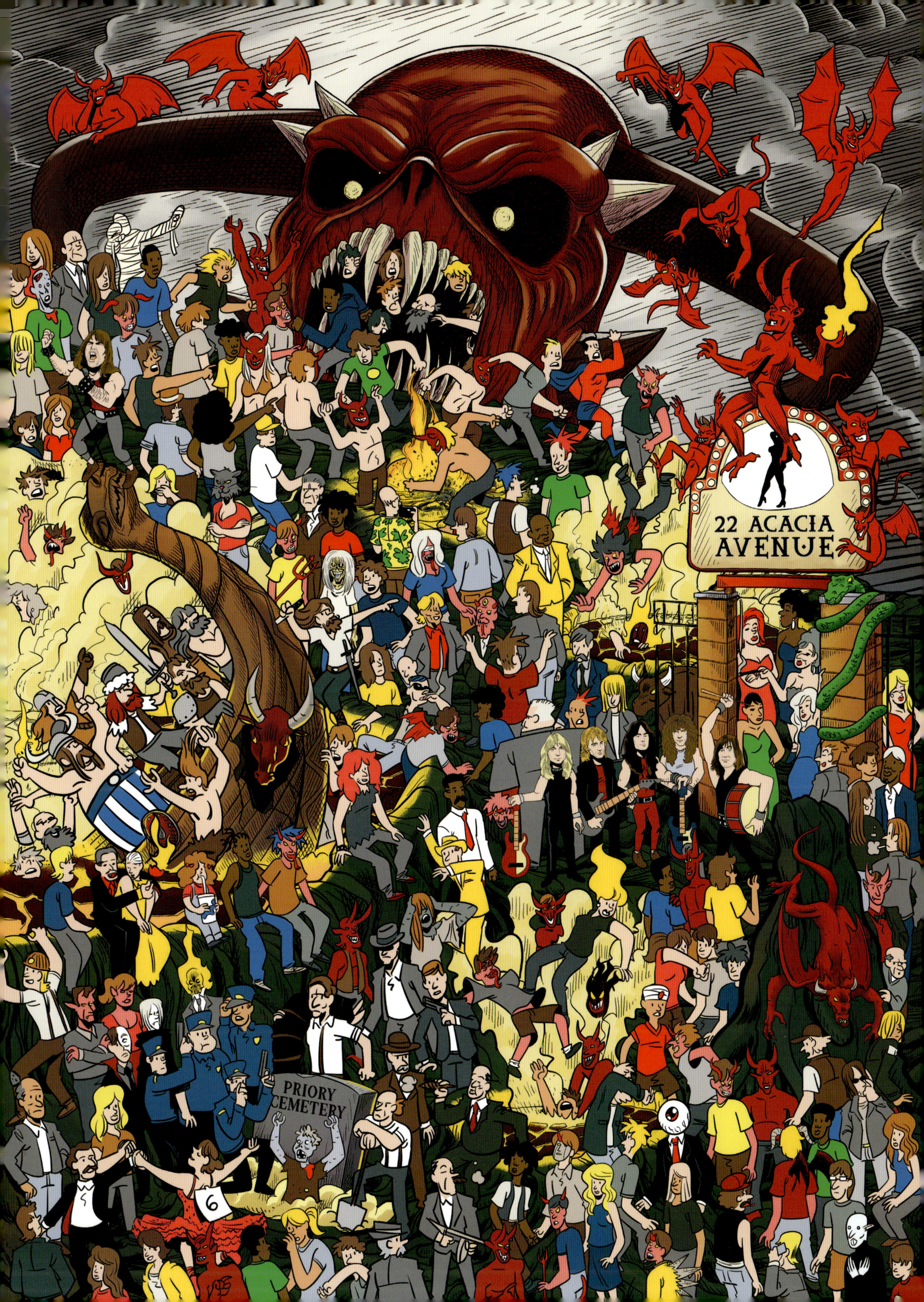
22 ACACIA
AVENUE
PRIORY
CEMETERY
6

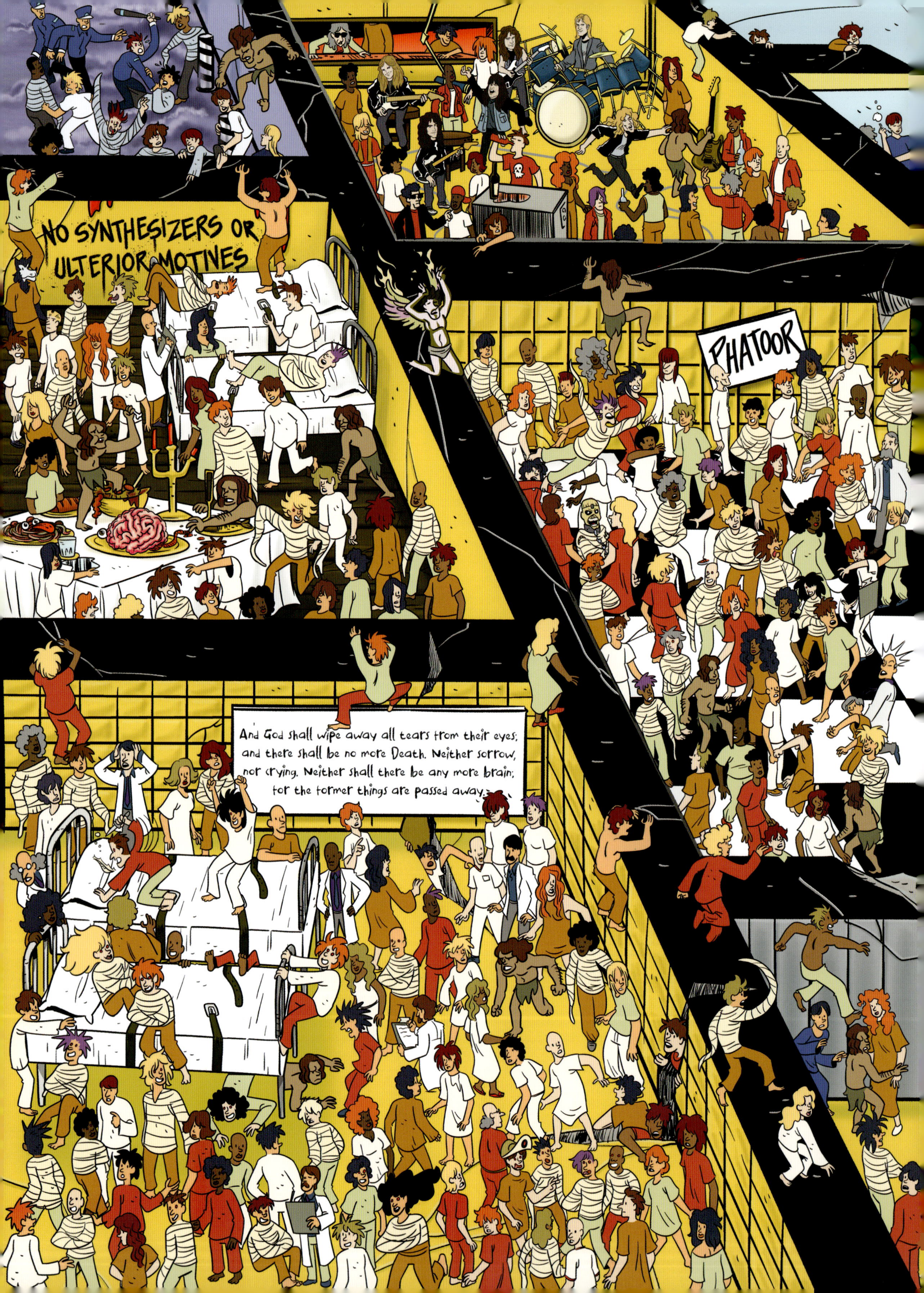
NO SYNTHESIZERS OR ULTERIOR MOTIVES
PHATOOR
And God shall wipe away all tears from their eyes; and there shall be no more Death. Neither sorrow, nor crying. Neither shall there be any more brain; for the former things are passed away.

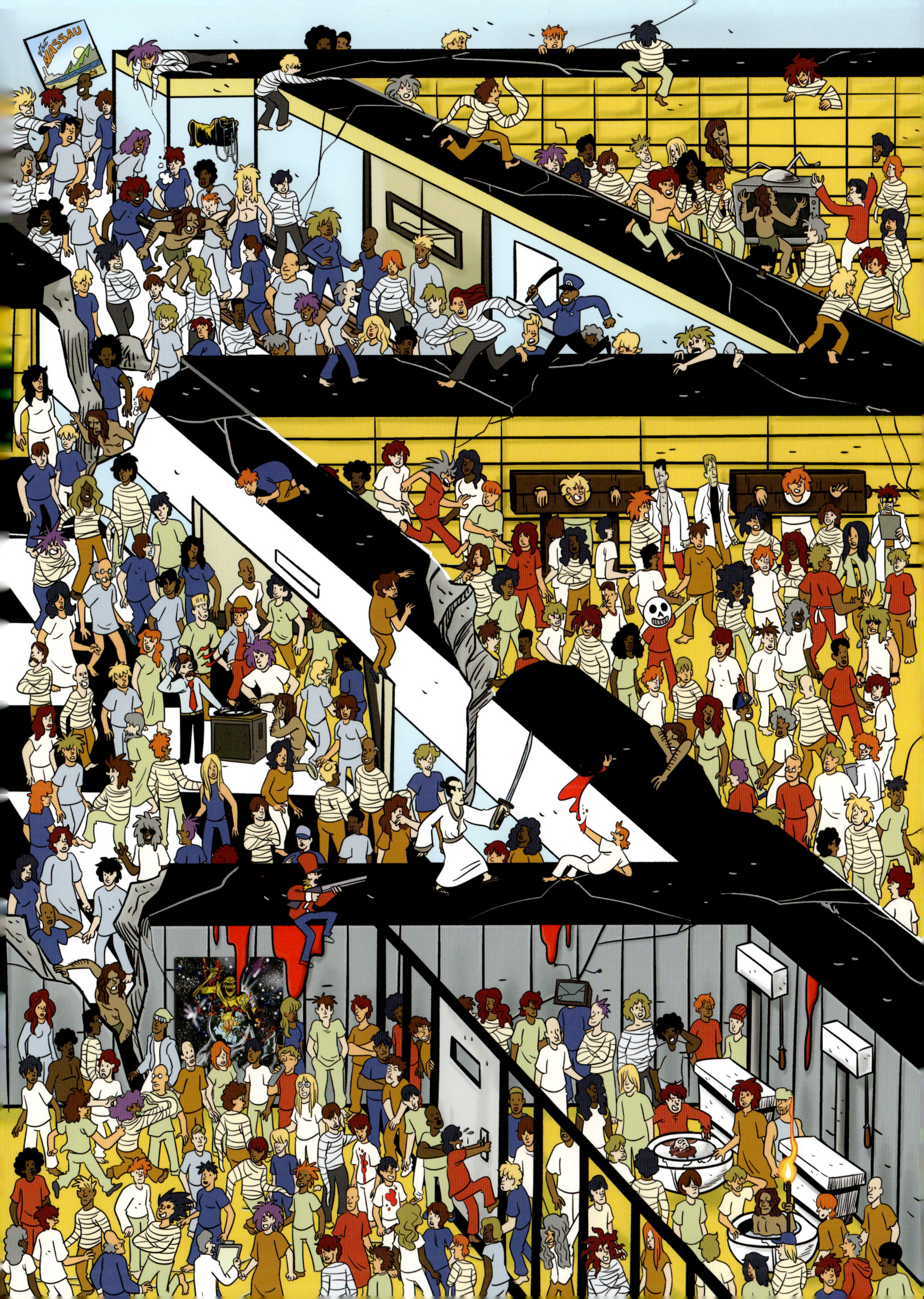
Visit
NASSAU

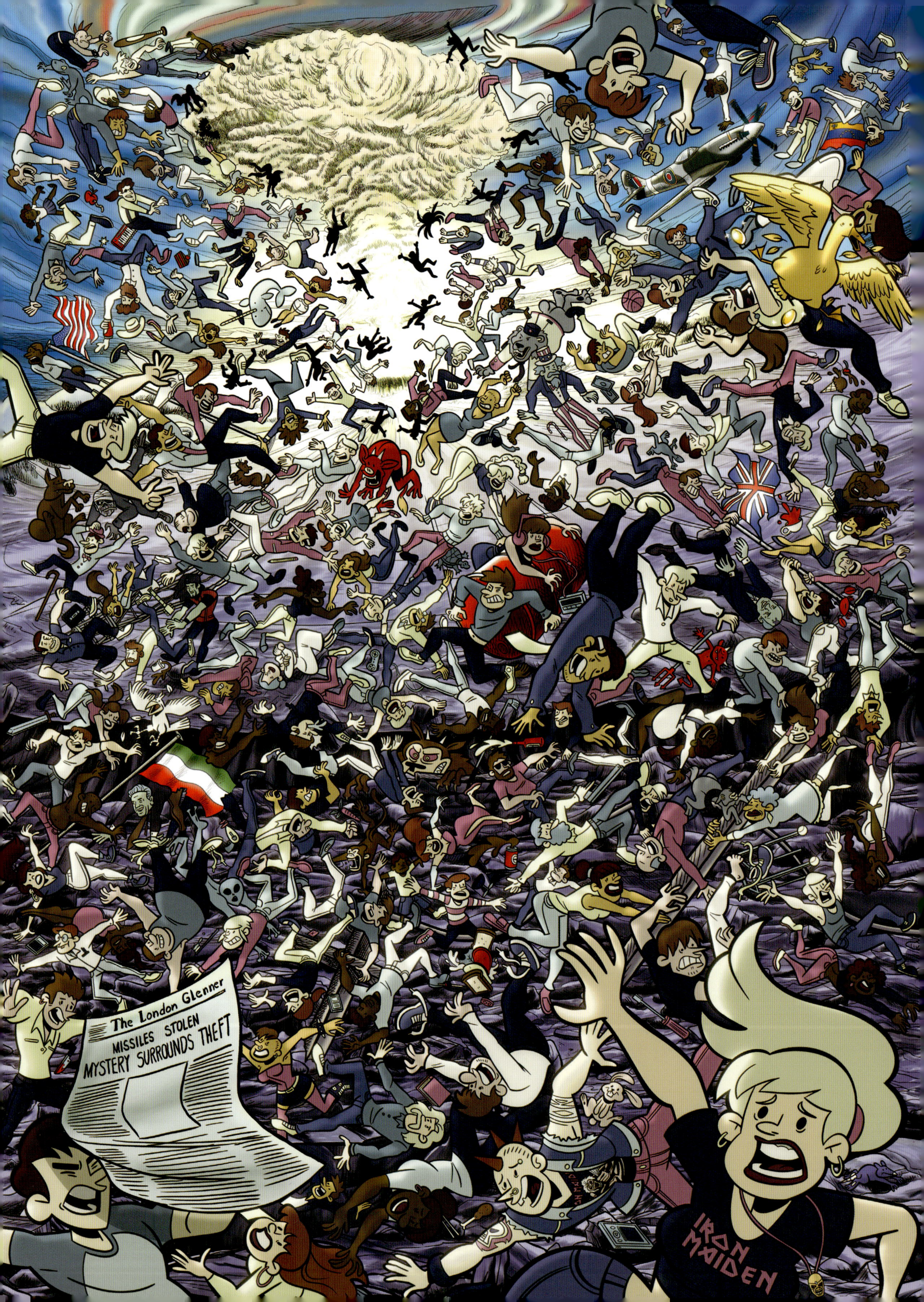
The London Glenner
MISSILES STOLEN
MYSTERY SURROUNDS THEFT
IRON MAIDEN

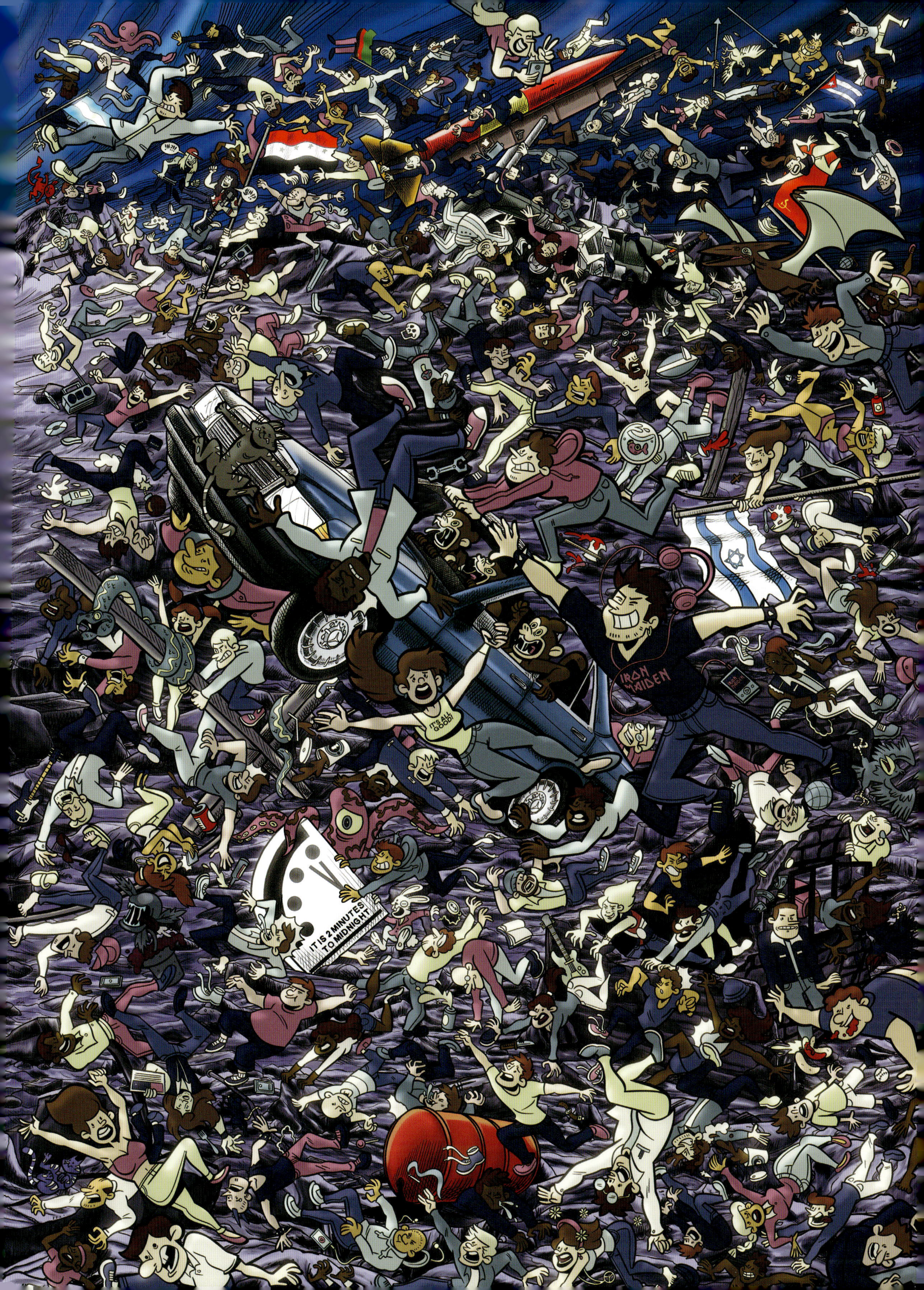
IRON MAIDEN
IT'S ALL GOOD!
IT IS 2 MINUTES TO MIDNIGHT

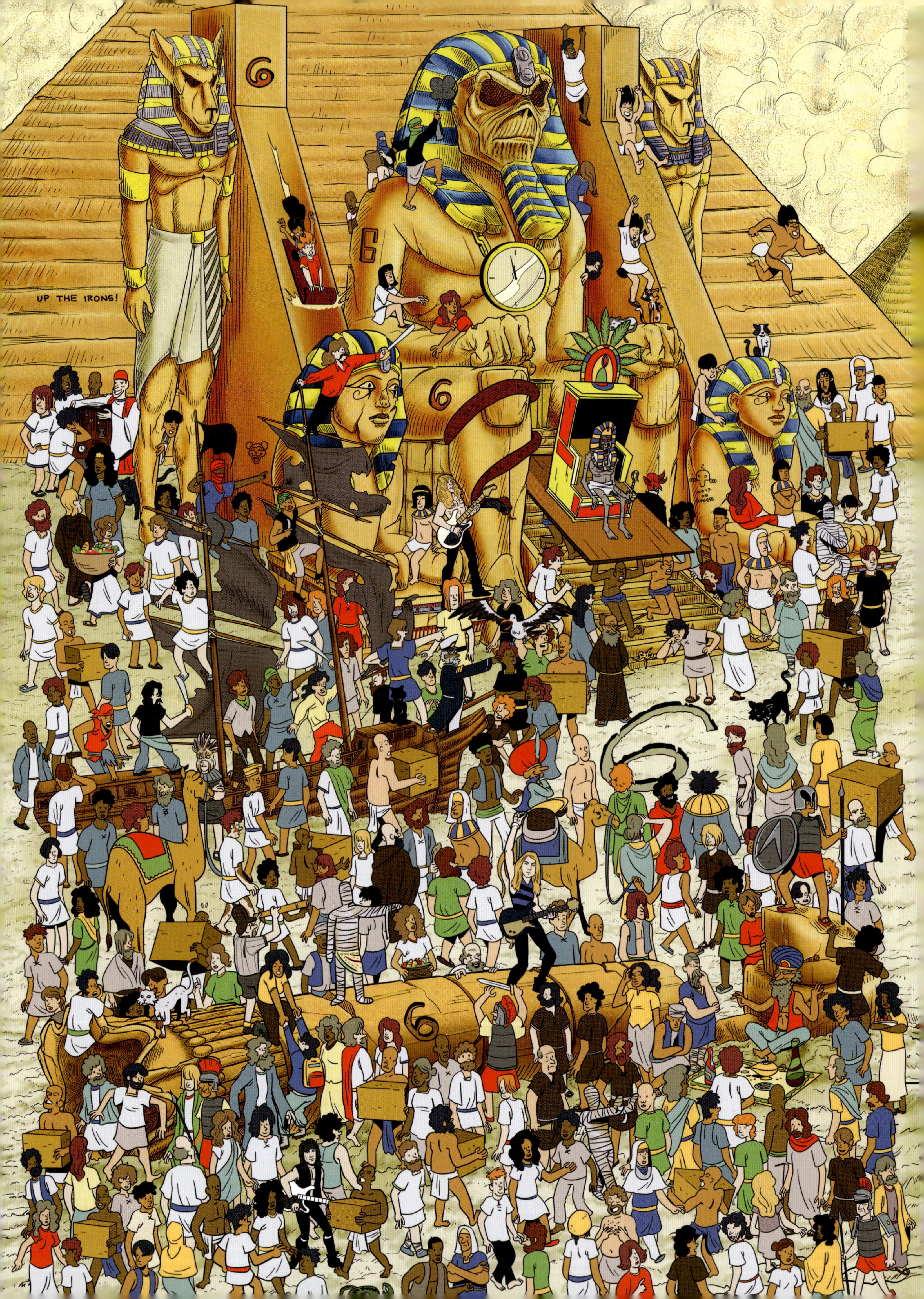

UP THE IRONS!
WOT? NO GUINESS

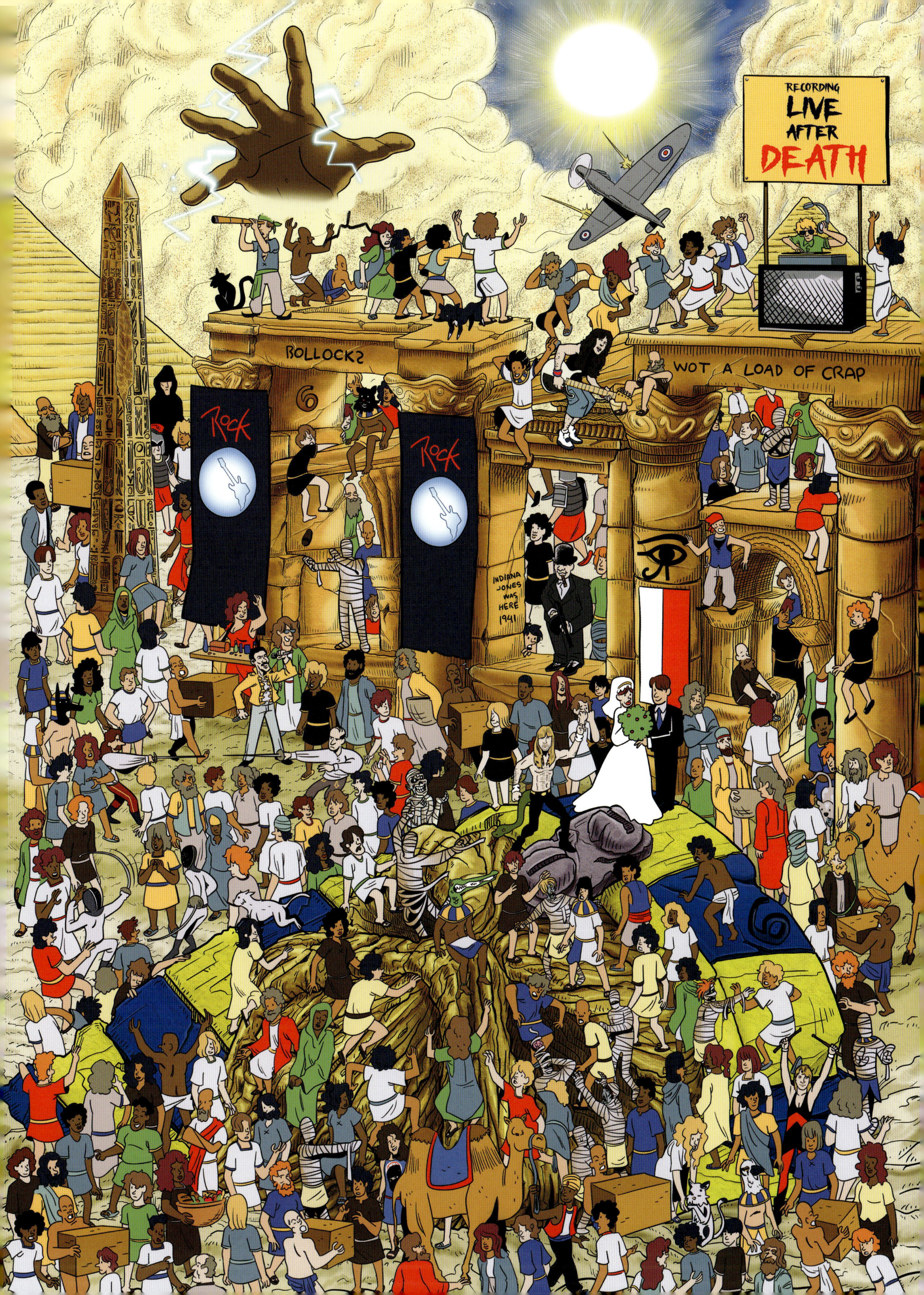
RECORDING
LIVE
AFTER
DEATH
BOLLOCKS
WOT A LOAD OF CRAP
6
ROCK
ROCK
INDIANA JONES WAS HERE 1941

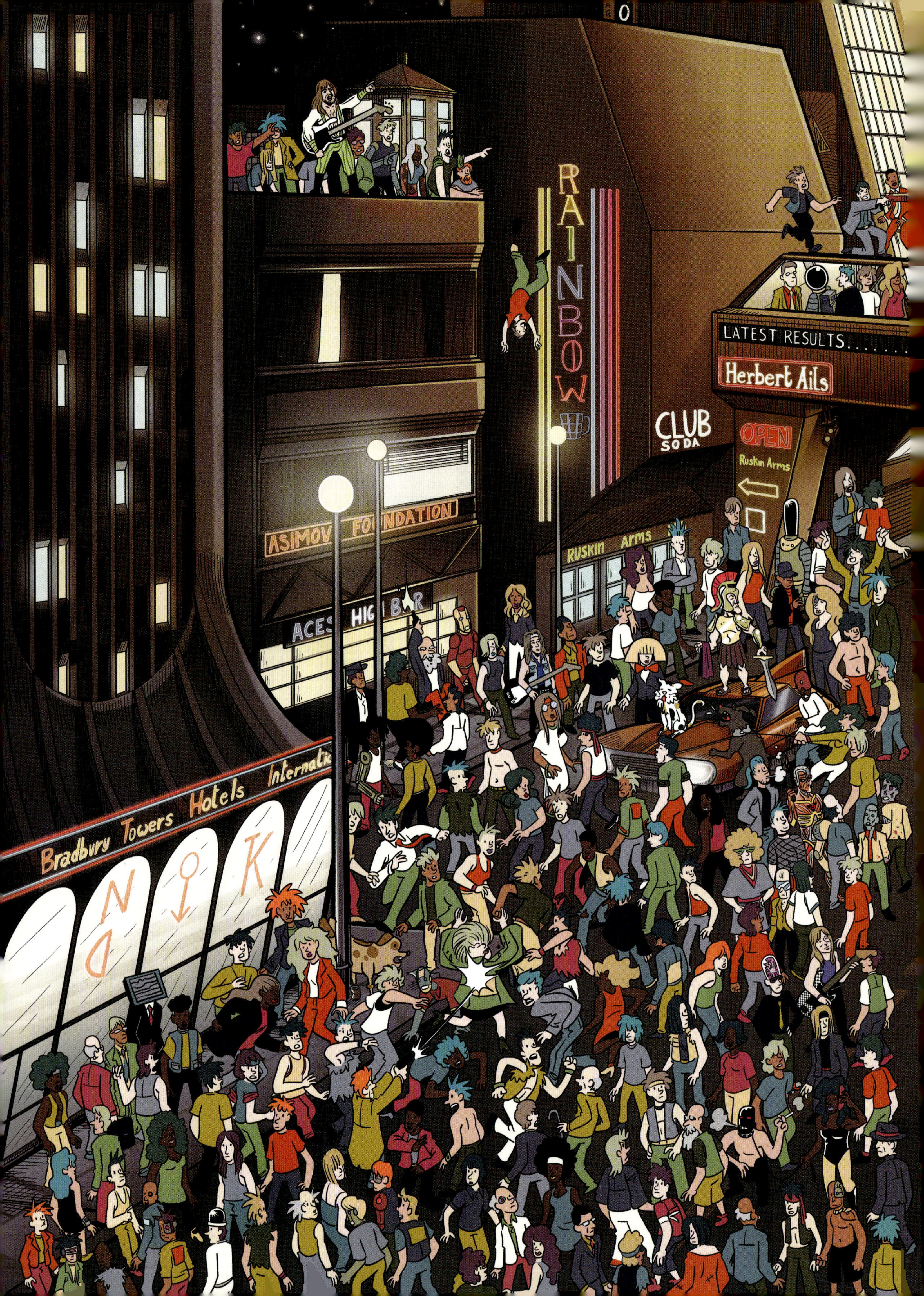
RAINBOW
LATEST RESULTS........
Herbert Ails
CLUB
SODA
OPEN
Ruskin Arms
RUSKIN Arms
ASIMOV FOUNDATION
ACES HIGH BAR
Bradbury Towers Hotels

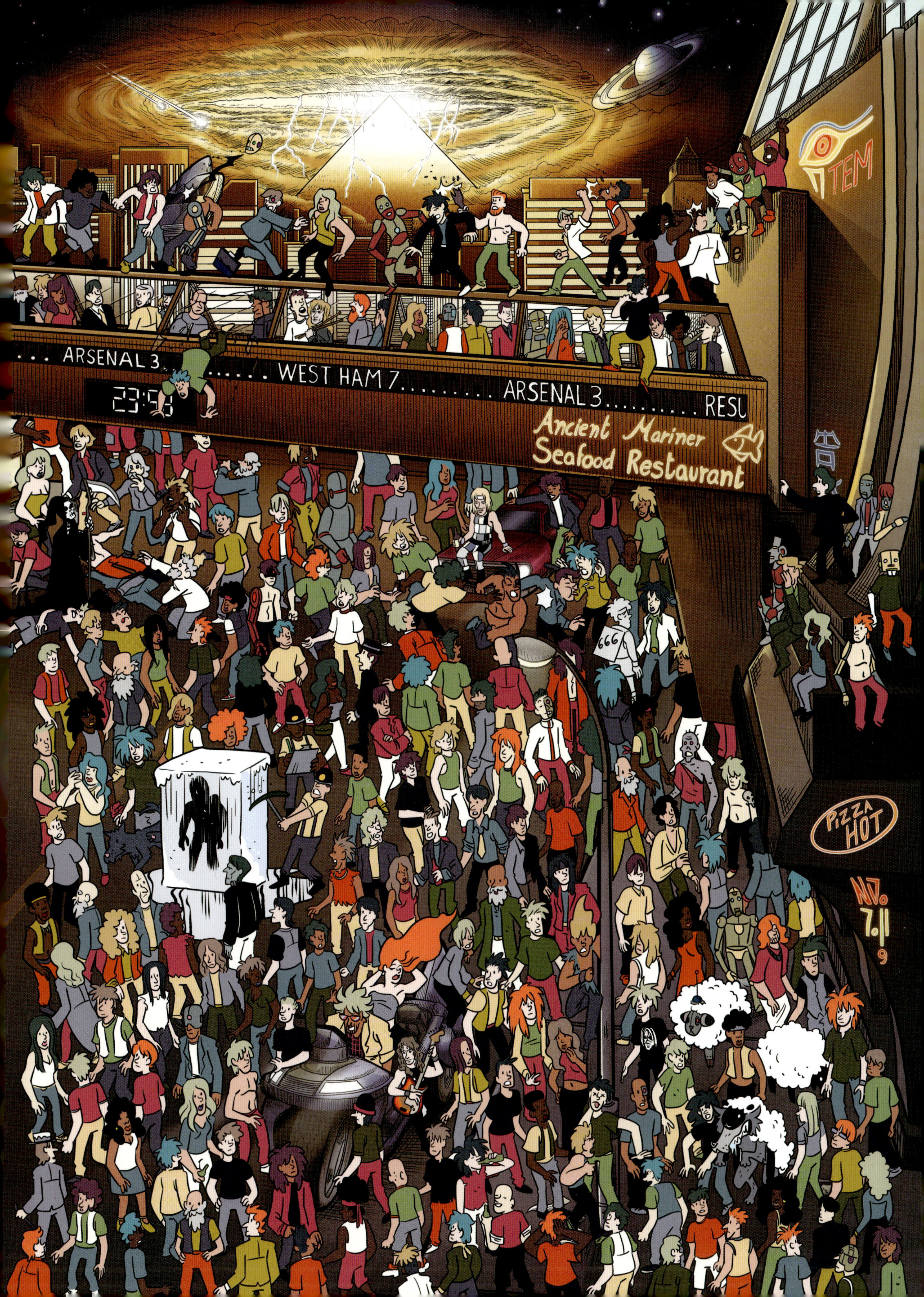

TEM
. . . ARSENAL 3. . . . . . . WEST HAM 7. . . . . ARSENAL 3. . . . . RESU
Ancient Mariner
Seafood Restaurant
666
PIZZA HOT

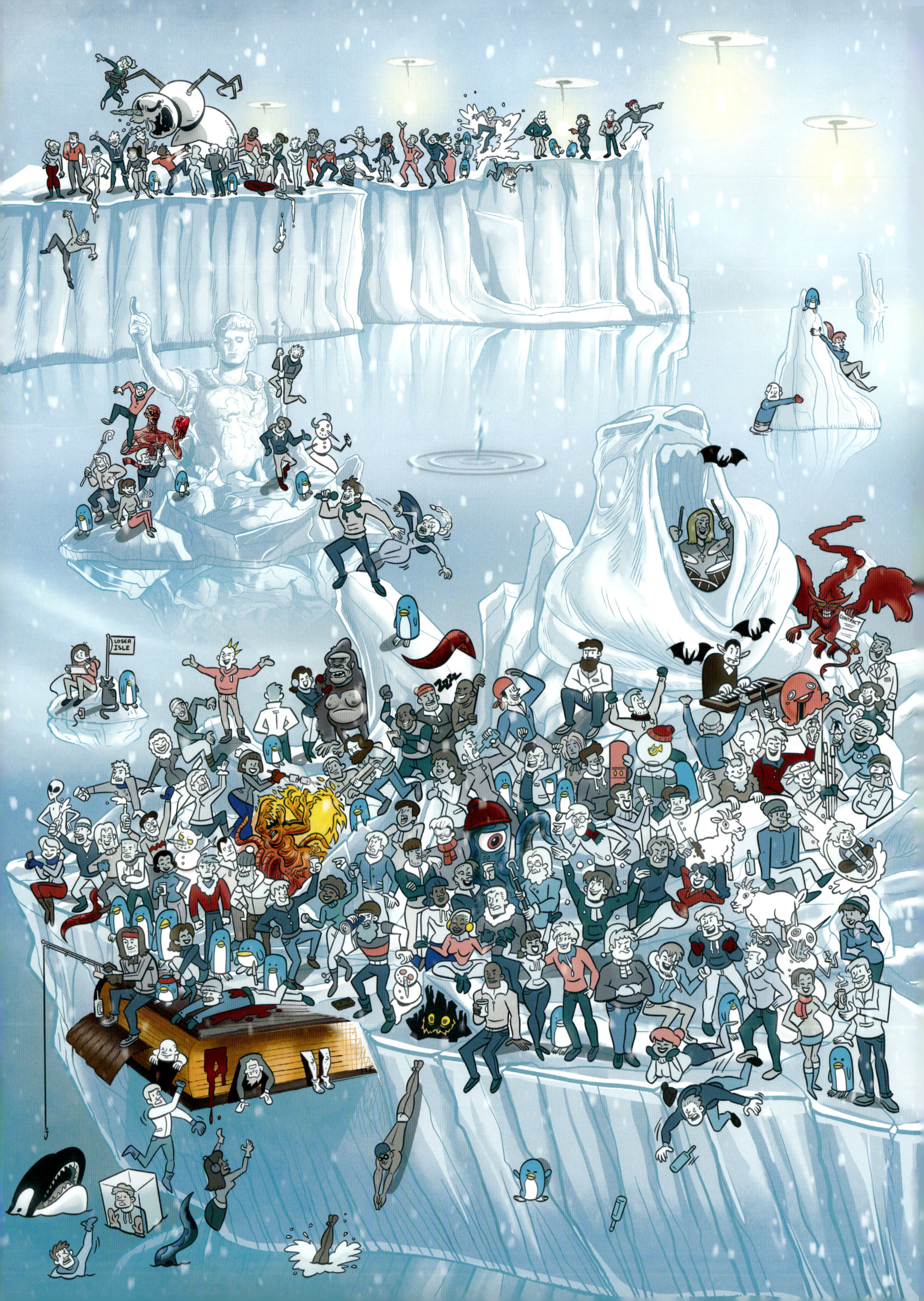
LOSER ISLE
CONTRACT

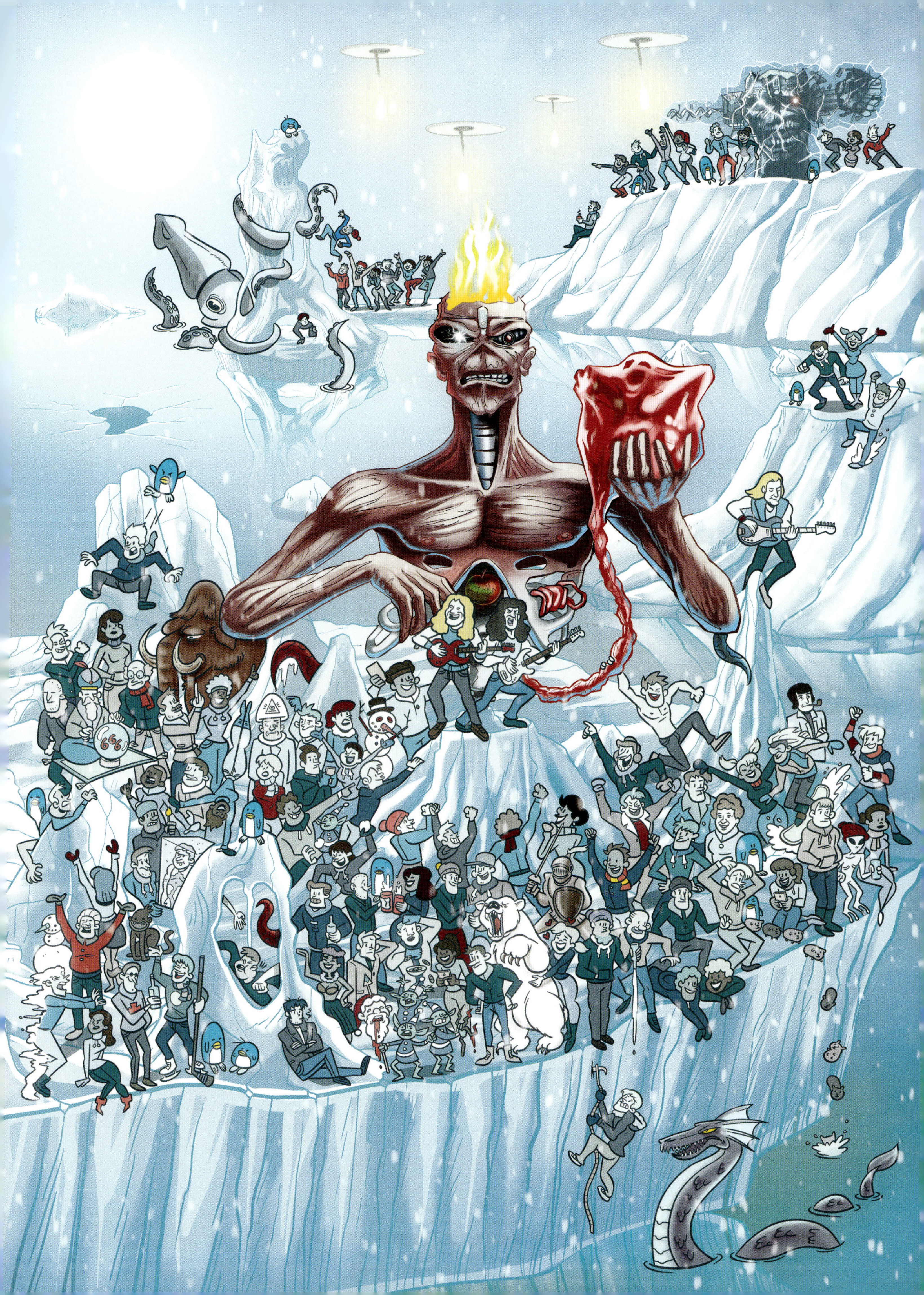

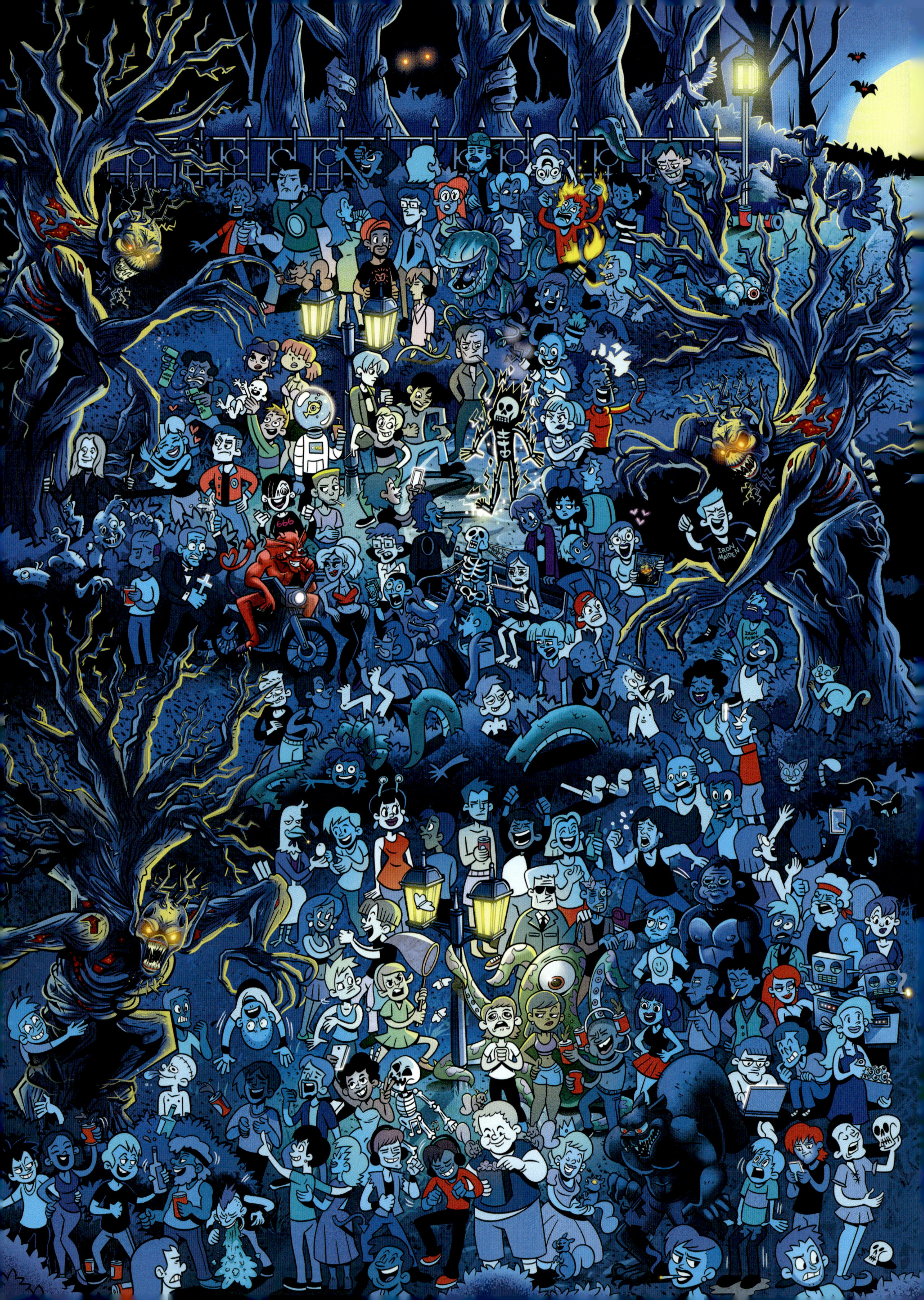
666
IRON MAIDEN

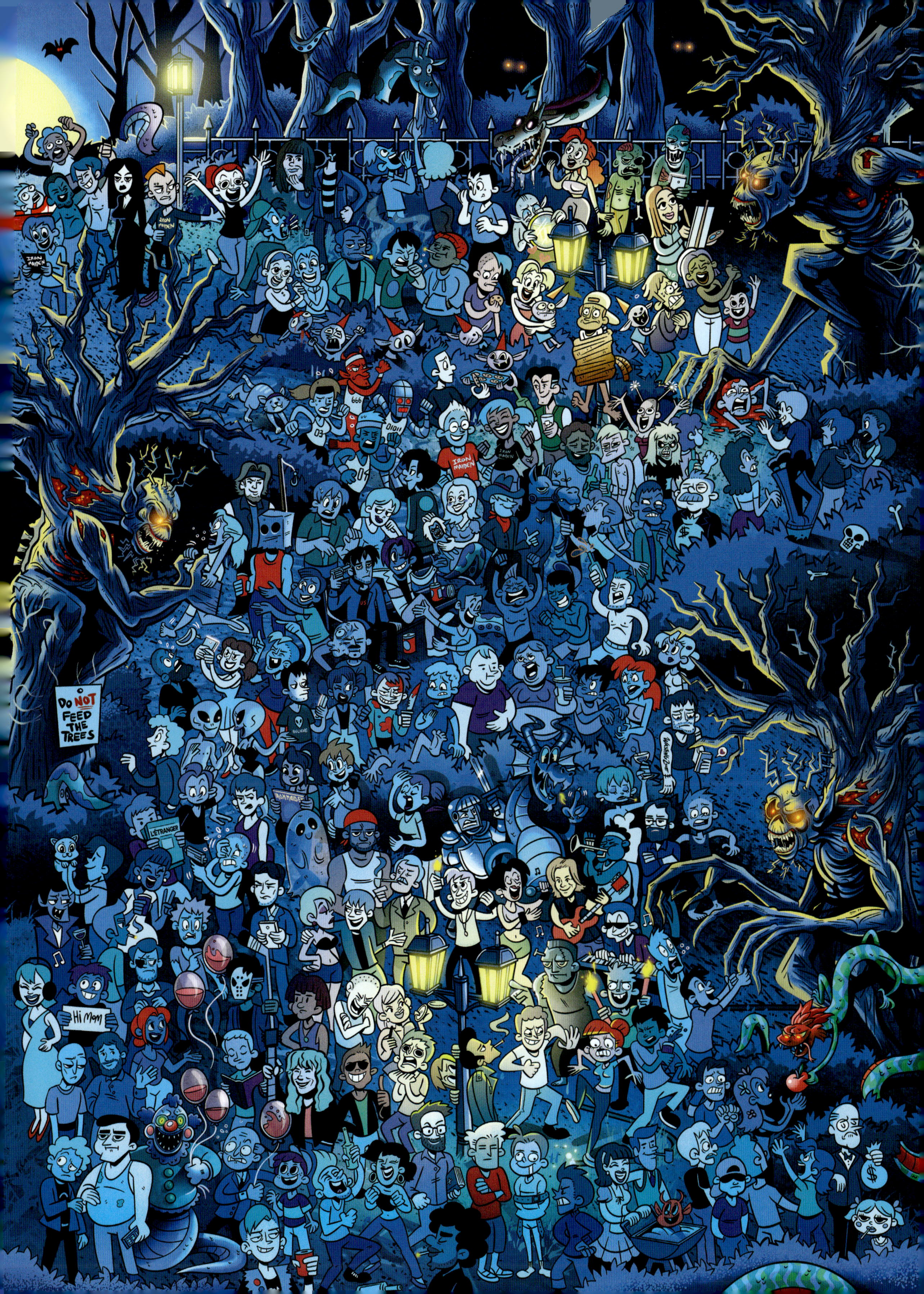
DO NOT FEED THE TREES
IRON MAIDEN
IRON MAIDEN
L'ÉTRANGER
Hi Mom

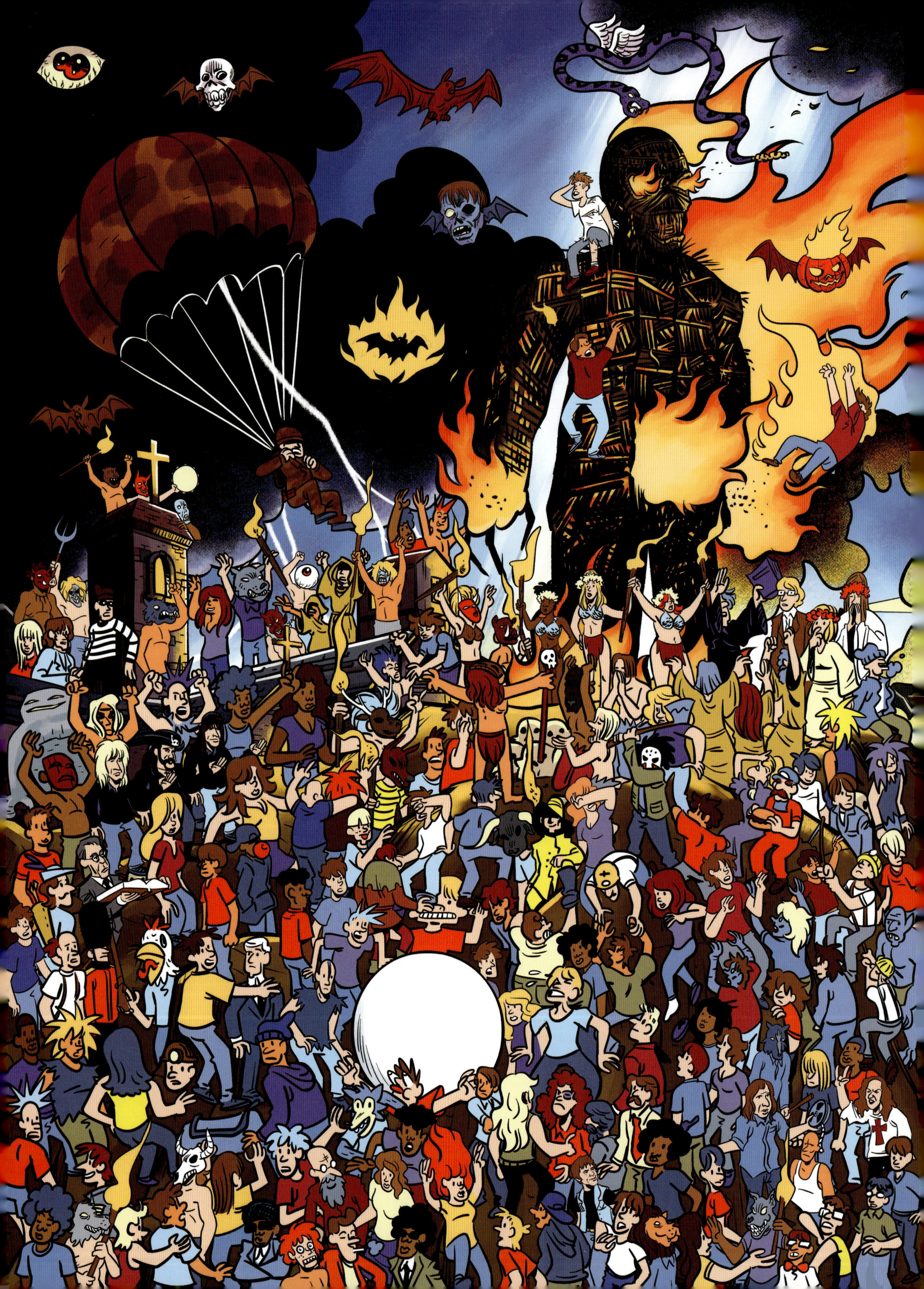

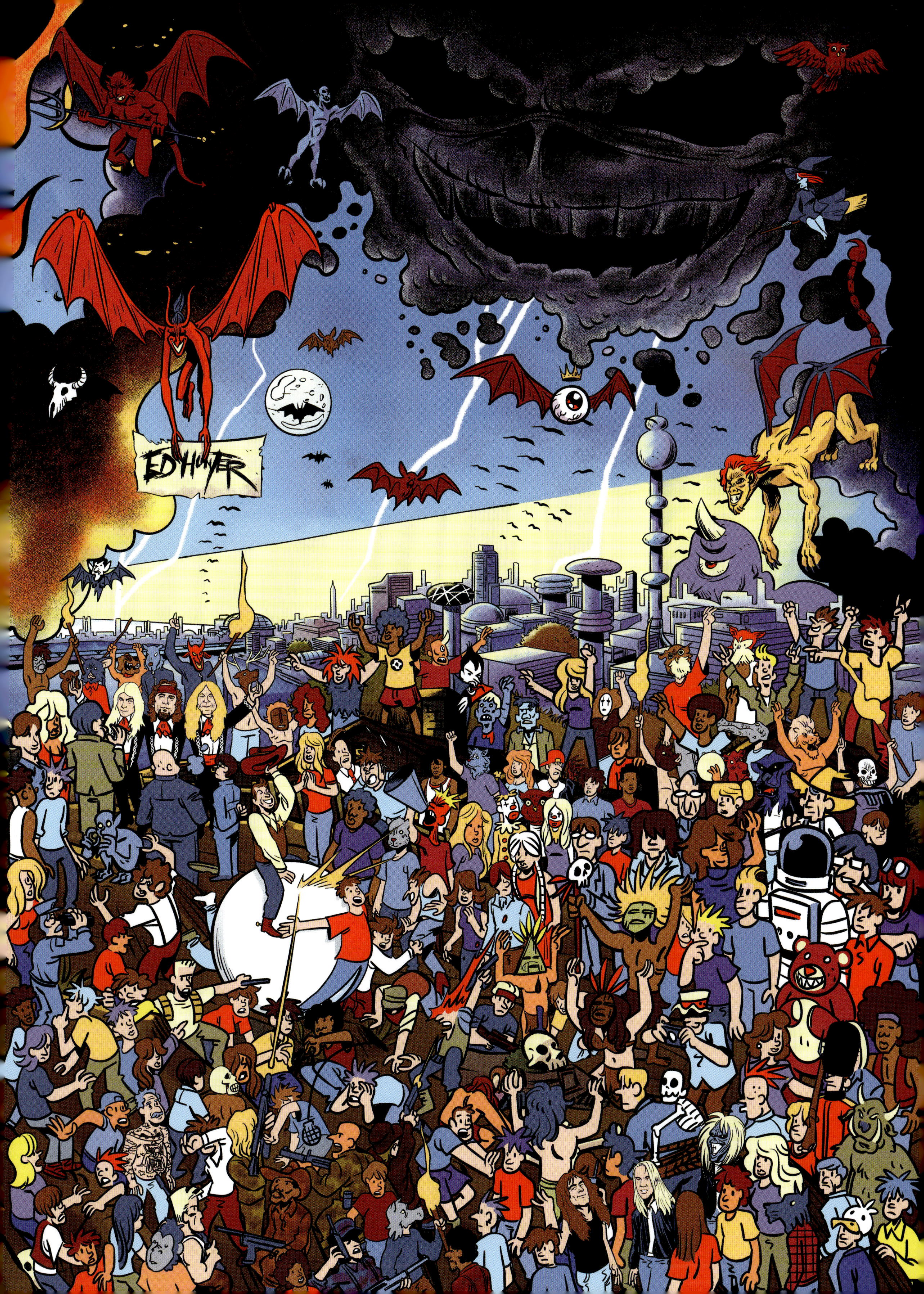
ED HUNTER

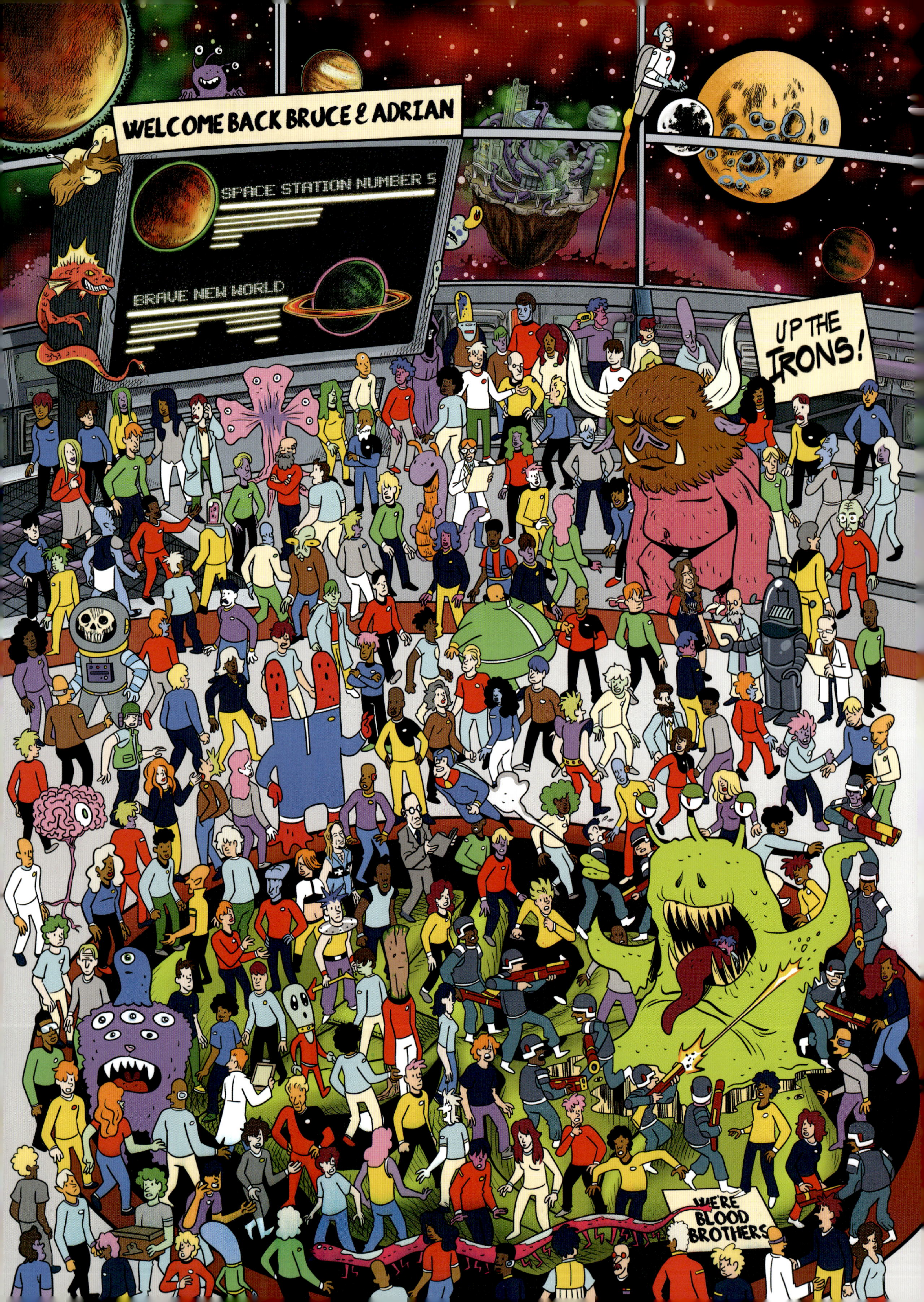
WELCOME BACK BRUCE & ADRIAN
SPACE STATION NUMBER 5
BRAVE NEW WORLD
UP THE IRONS!
WE'RE BLOOD BROTHERS

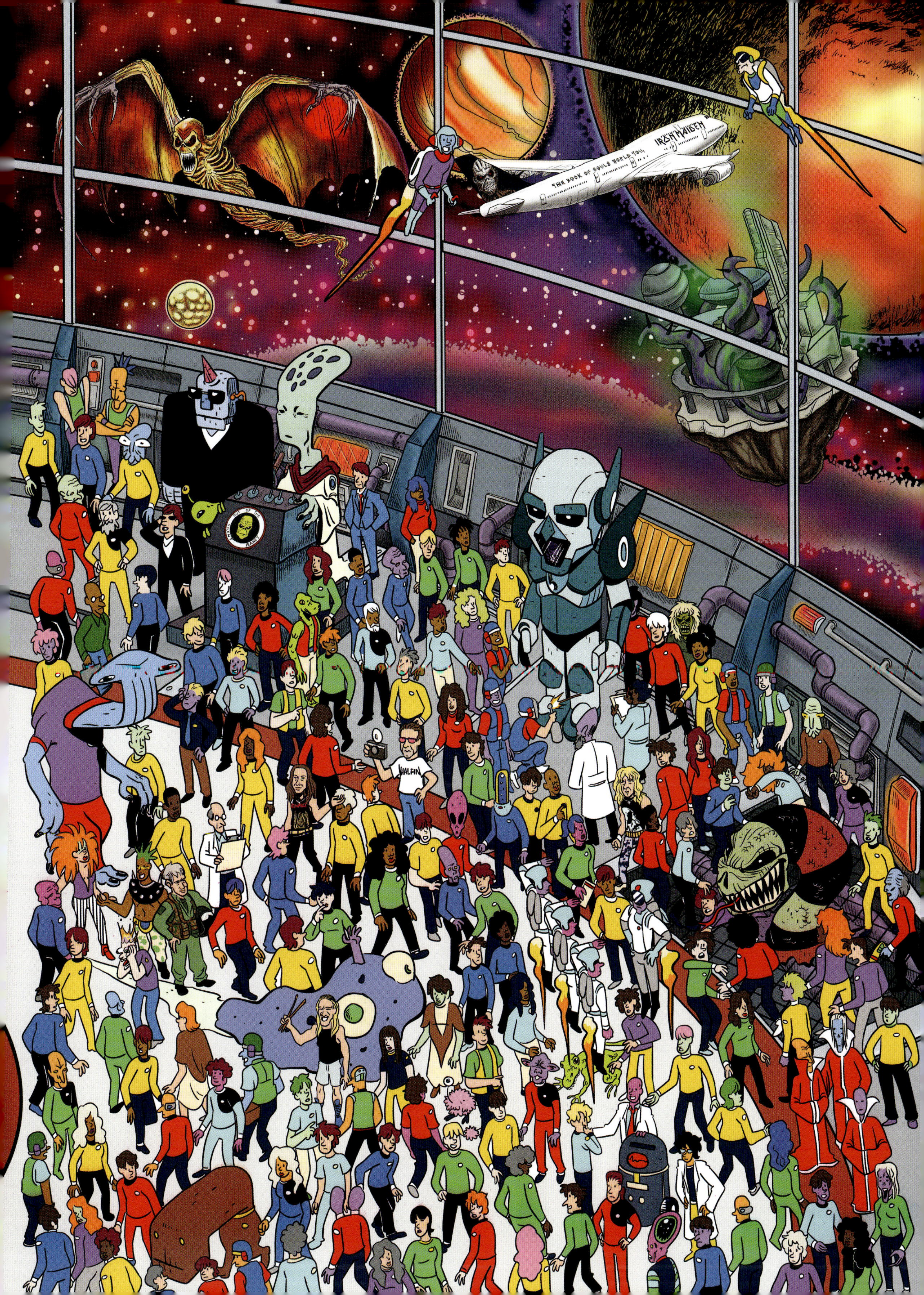
IRON MAIDEN
THE BOOK OF SOULS WORLD TOU
HALFIN

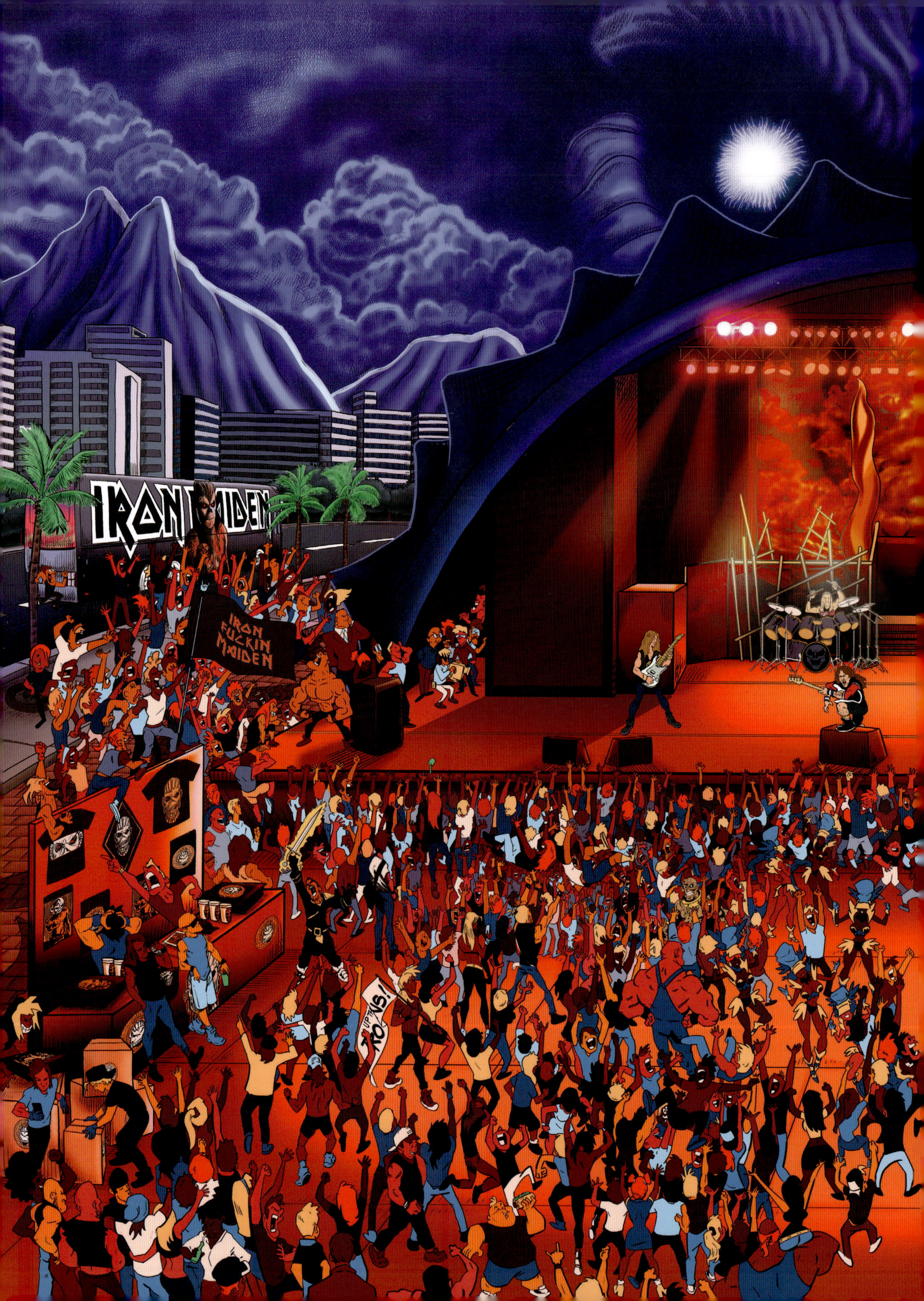
IRON
FUCKIN
MAIDEN

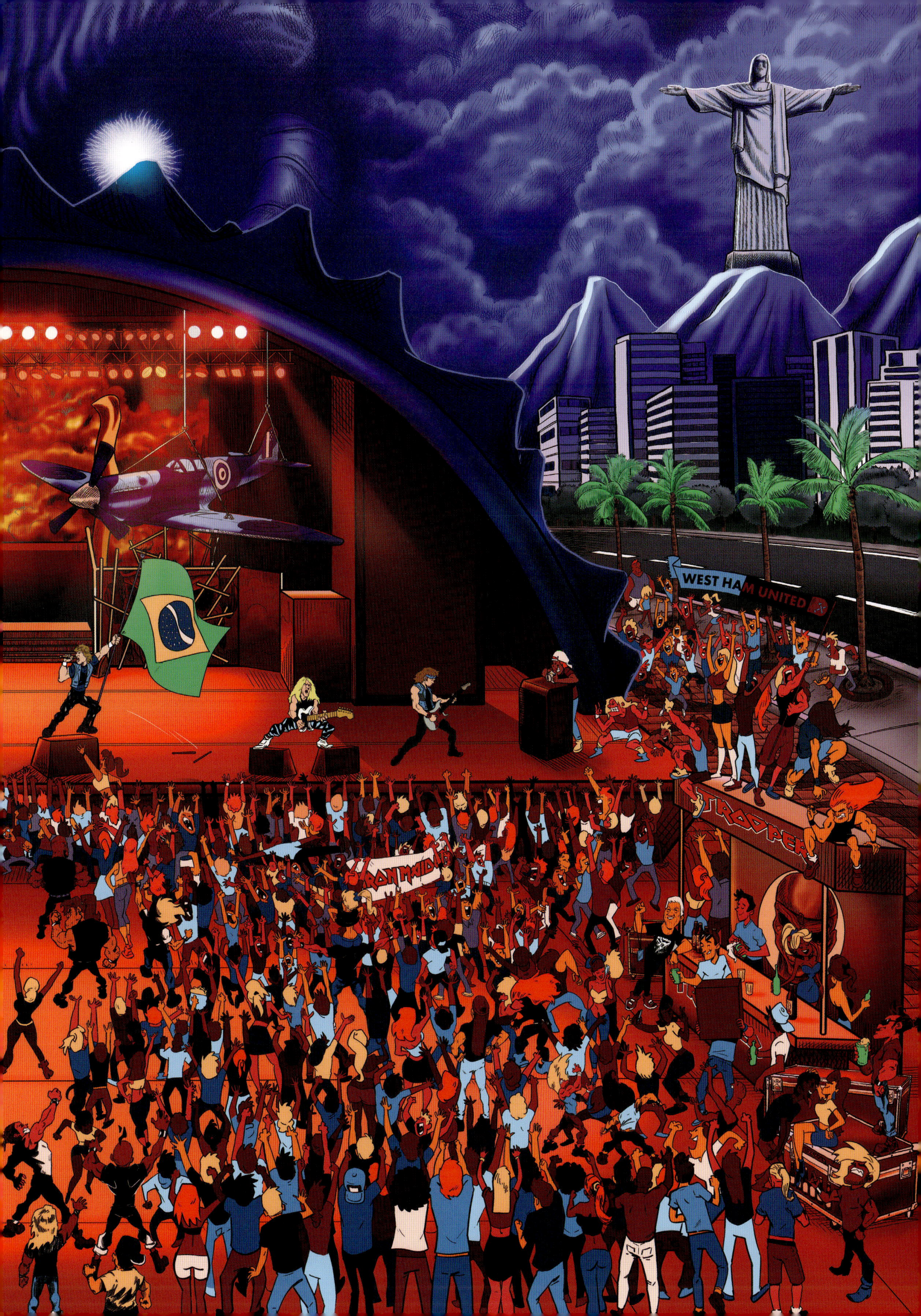
WEST HAM UNITED

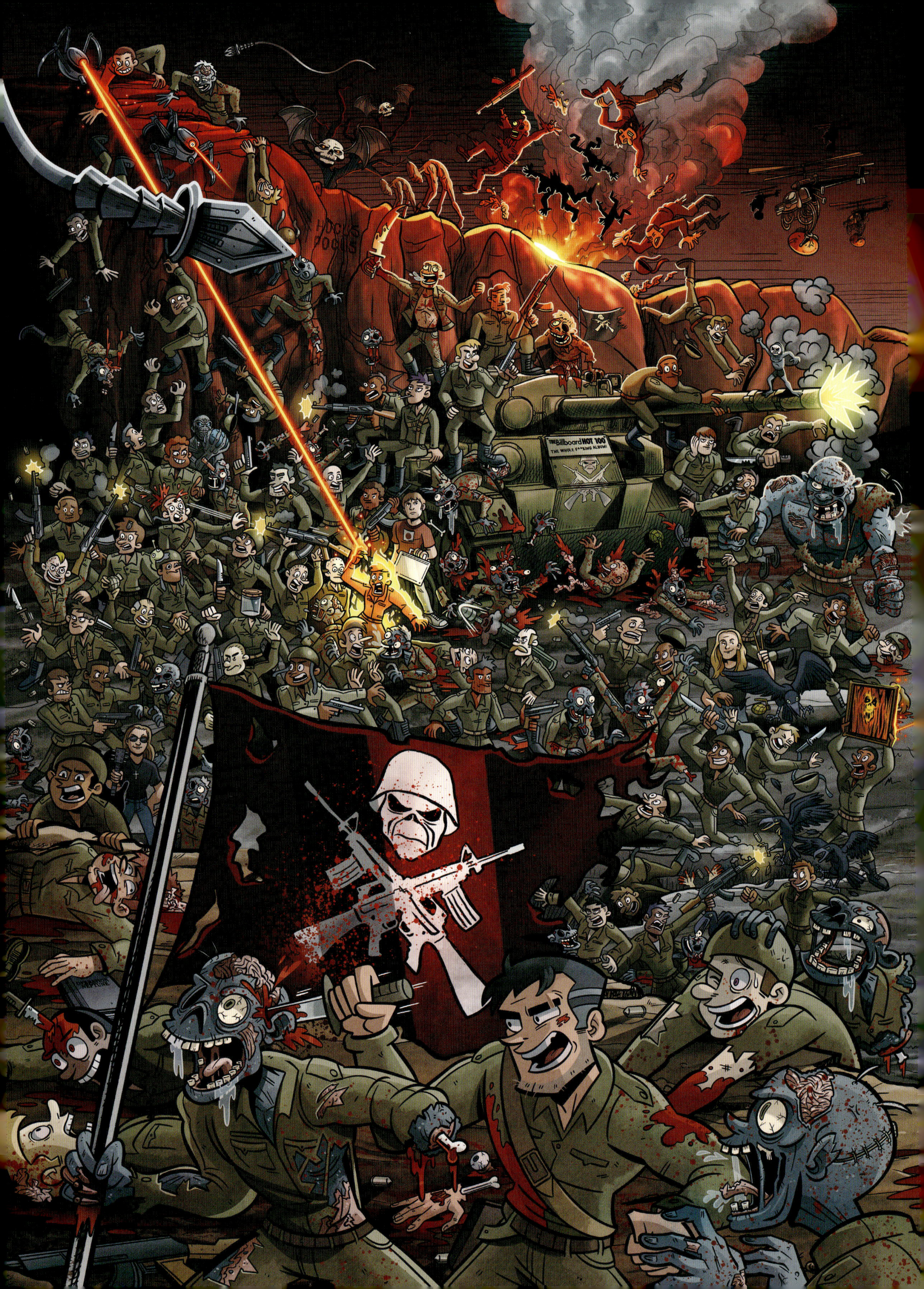
HOCUS POCUS
THE Billboard HOT 100
THE WHOLE F**KING ALBUM!

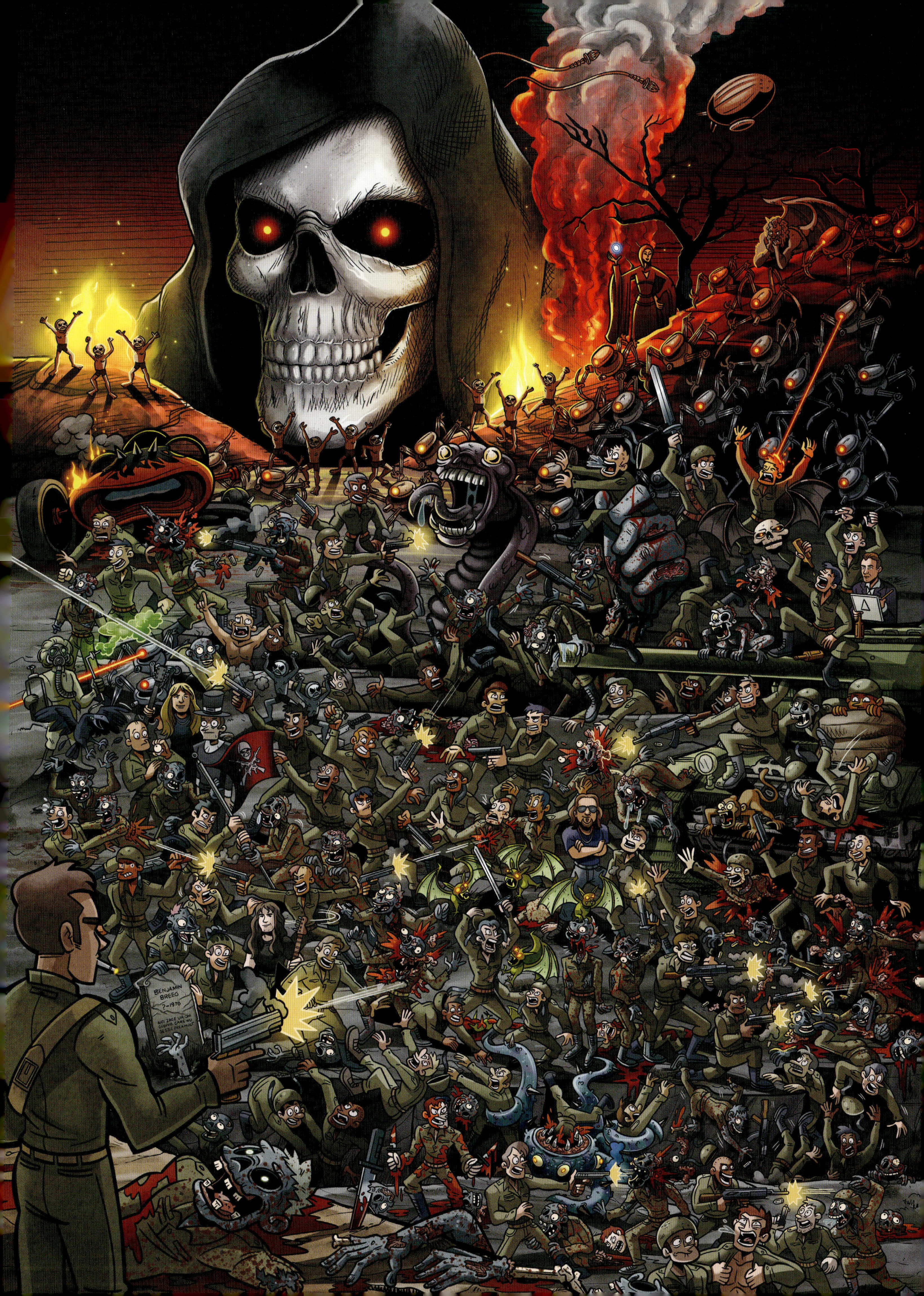
BENJAMIN BREEG
?-1978
A

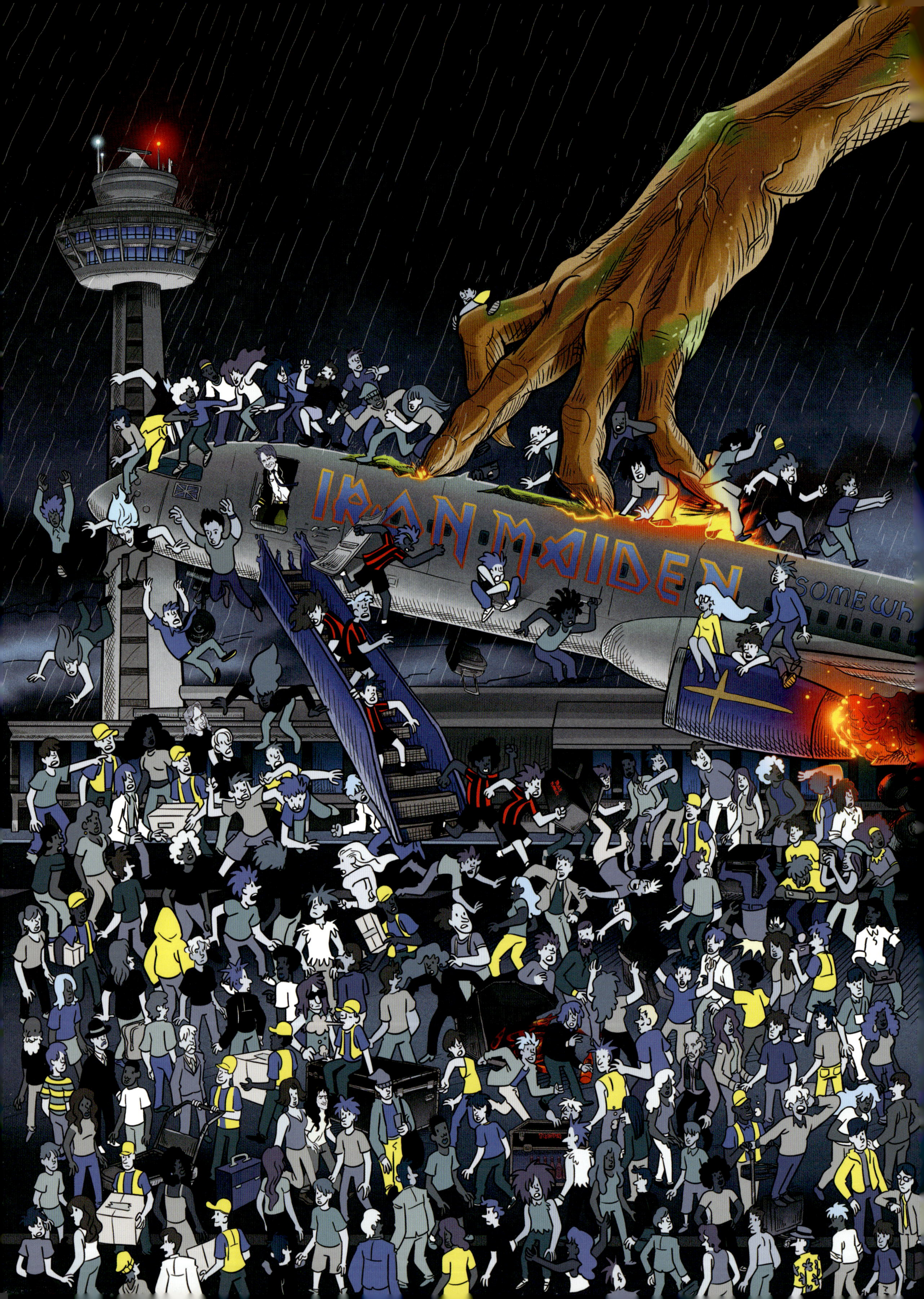
IRON MAIDEN
SOMEWH

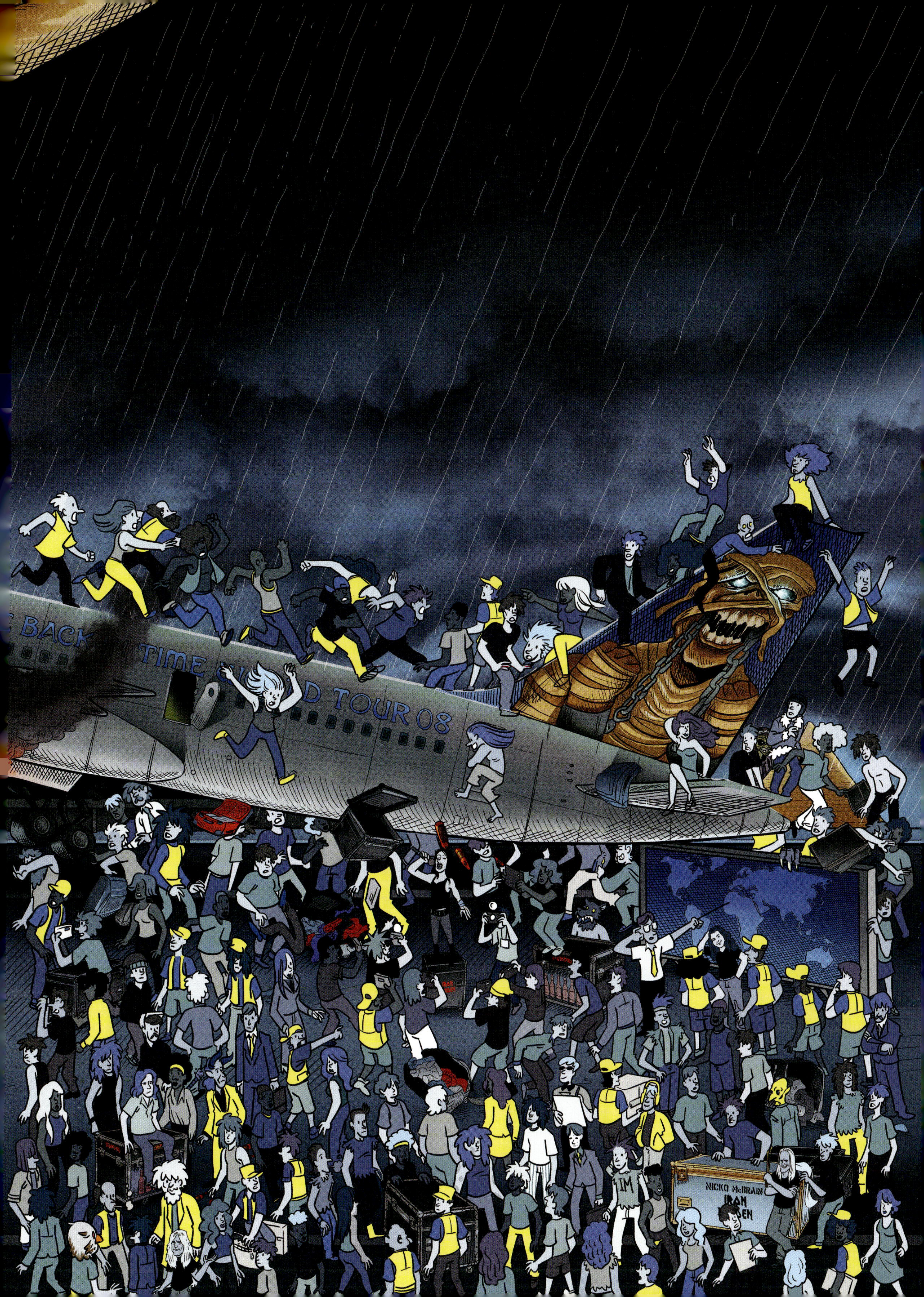
BACK
TIME
D TOUR 08
NICKO McBRAIN
IRAN

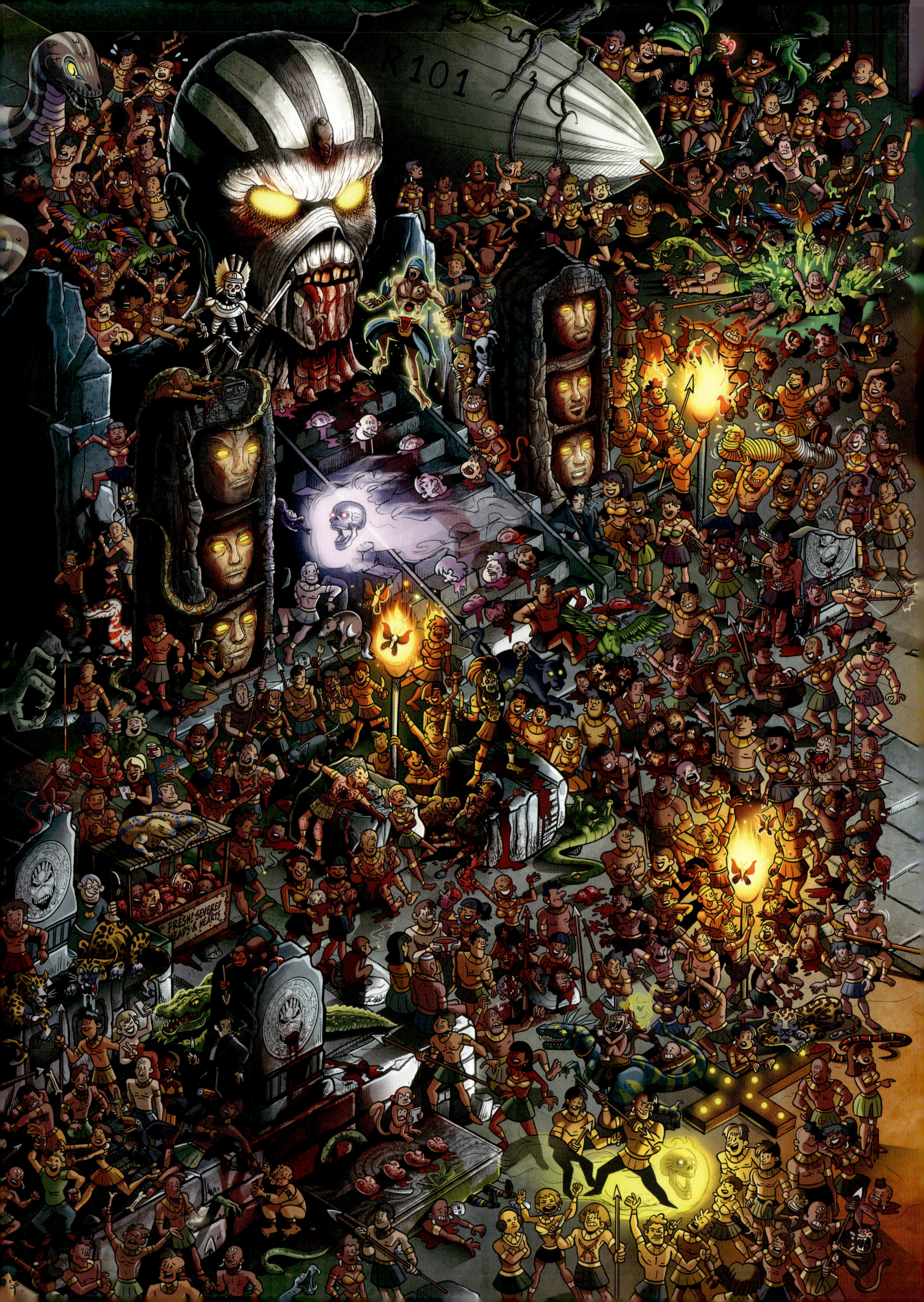
R101
FRESH! SEVERED
HEADS & HEARTS

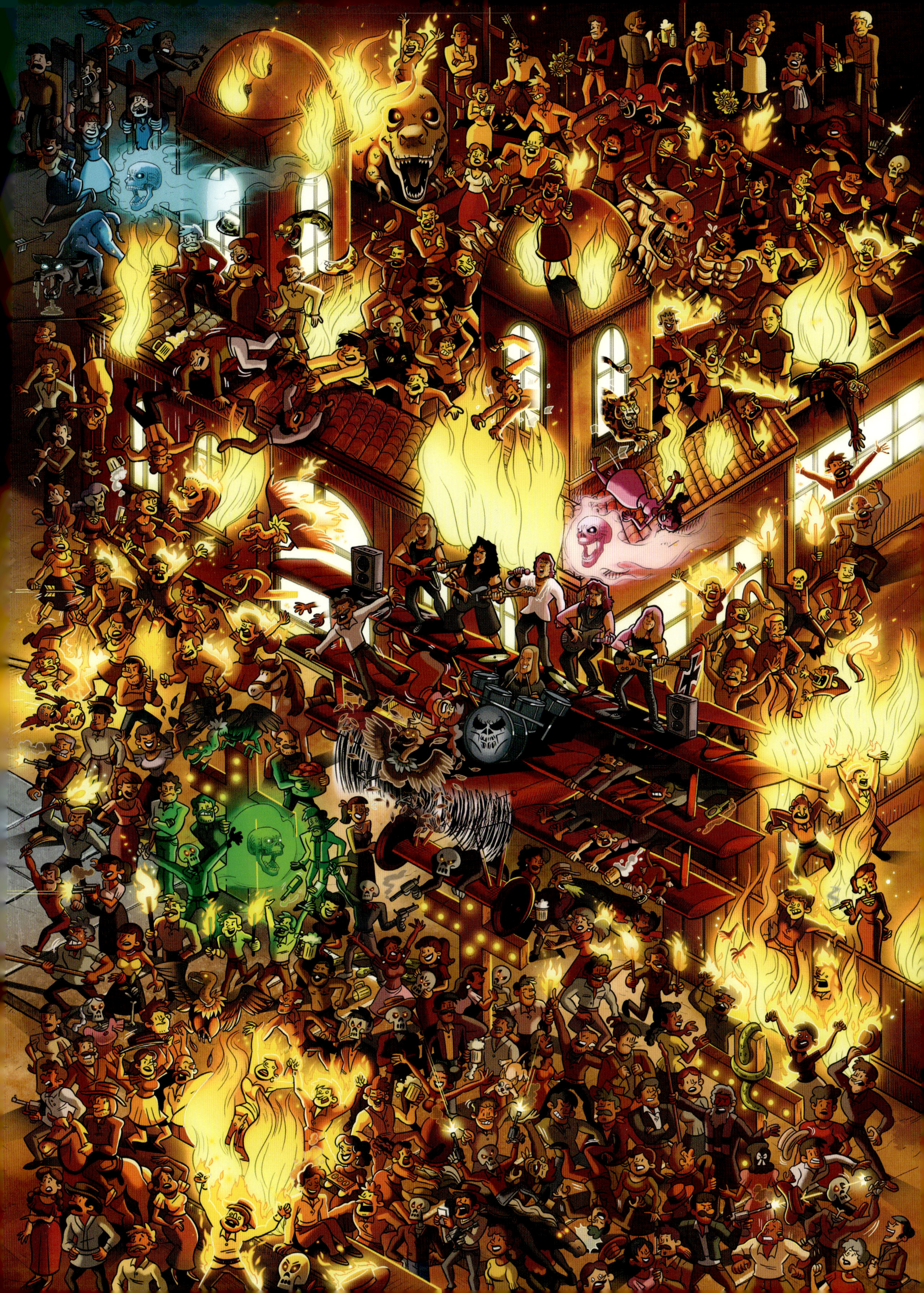

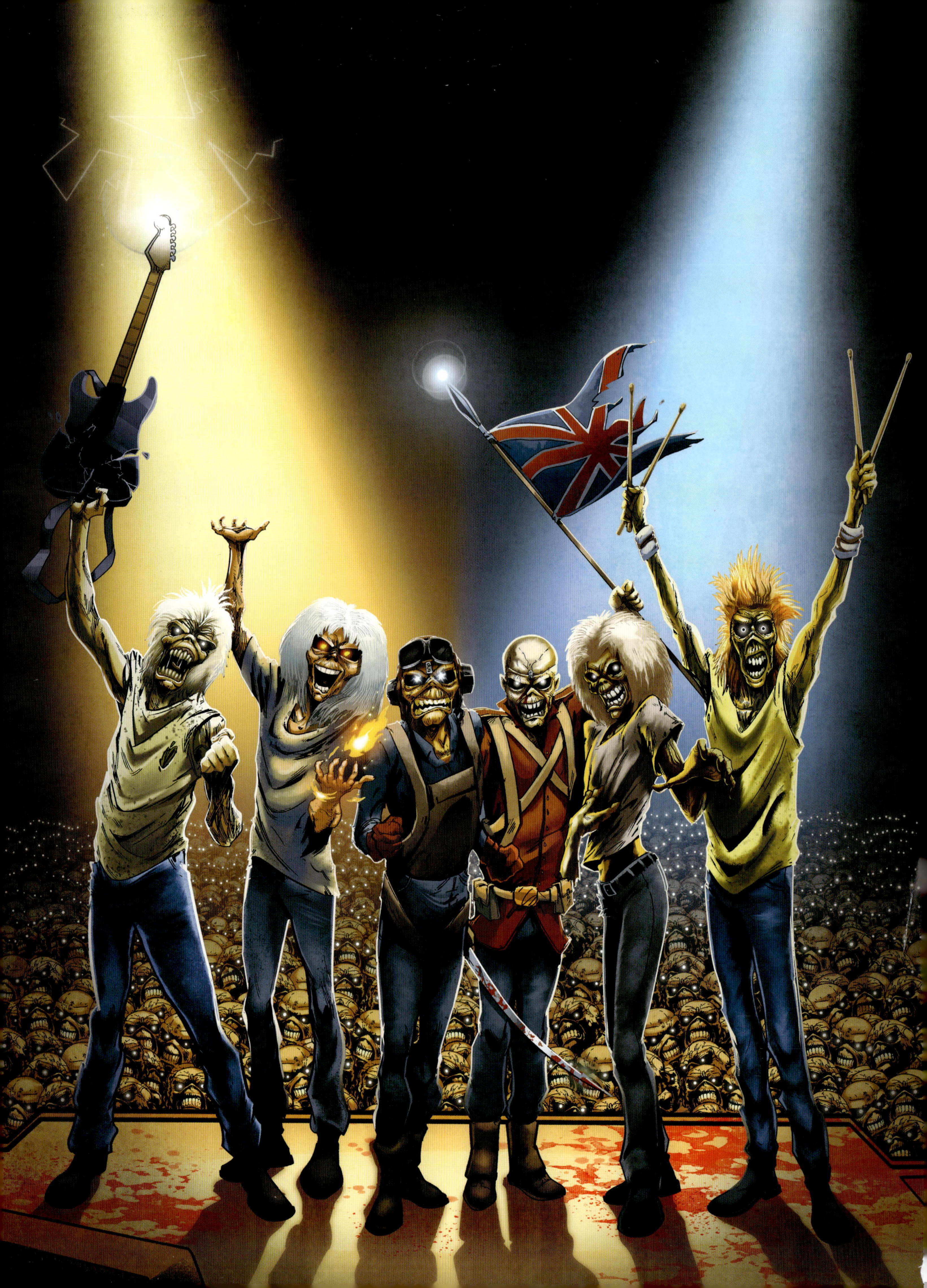